A HI...   IIAN SPORT

POMEGRANATE ARTBOOKS SAN FRANCISCO

£8.95

FIRST PUBLISHED DEPICTION OF SURFING, FROM WILLIAM ELLIS'S *POLYNESIAN RESEARCHES*, 1831

Surfing

A History of the Ancient Hawaiian Sport

Dedicated to the Hawaiian Surfer

Published by Pomegranate Artbooks
P.O. Box 6099
Rohnert Park, CA 94927

Library of Congress Cataloging-in-Publication Data

Finney, Ben R.
           Surfing : a history of the ancient Hawaiian sport / Ben Finney and
           James D. Houston.
                  p. cm.
           Rev. ed. of: Surfing, the sport of Hawaiian kings. [1966].
           Includes bibliographical references.
           ISBN 0-87654-594-0 (pbk.)
           1. Surfing—Hawaii—History. I. Houston, James D.   II. Finney, Ben R.
           Surfing, the sport of Hawaiian kings.   III. Title.
  GV840.28F55   1996
  797.3'2'09969—dc20   95-52233
                                    CIP

Pomegranate catalog no. A832
Designed by Tim Lewis
Printed in Korea

00   99   98   97   96   5   4   3   2   1

CONTENTS

ONE OF THE FIRST KNOWN PHOTOGRAPHS OF A SURFER WITH HIS BOARD,
C. 1890. PHOTO COURTESY BISHOP MUSEUM, HONOLULU.

Foreword

The more things change, it has often been said, the more they remain the same. And so it is with the world of surfing, which in some ways has changed enormously in the years since this book was first published in 1966.

A simple device like the ankle-leash, for example, has eliminated the long swims that used to consume half of every surfer's energy and time in the water. And thanks to continuous experiments with board design, maneuvers are possible now that surfers in the mid 1960s could only dream about. Consider the arrival of the "Short Board." Few surfers had seen a board less than nine or ten feet long, the standard length since soon after World War II. And those ten-foot boards had been a great liberation from the unwieldy planks of the 1930s. The boards that began to appear on beaches in the late sixties harked back to a shorter version the early Hawaiians had called *alaia*—seven, six, sometimes five feet long. With these new models came later take-offs, more radical turns, and virtuoso stunts like a 360-degree whirl in the midst of a high-speed ride.

Meanwhile, thanks to the ongoing spirit of adventure, enhanced by the insulating pleasures of the wetsuit, surfers have tried waves along just about every surfable coastline on the planet, from Costa Rica to Bali's Kuta Beach, from Tierra del Fuego to British Columbia and beyond. As both a sport and an industry, surfing is now more internationalized than ever, with a professional circuit and contests staged around the world.

And yet, for all the advances in equipment and technique, certain elemental features haven't changed much at all. The forces that cause inviting swells to hump offshore are the same as they have been for countless millennia—the inexorable push of wind and water. From island to island, from continent to continent, the same reefs still wait submerged. Day after day surfers jockey for position as a wave rises to block out half the sky. They paddle hard and feel the rush and lift of nature's mysterious power, leap to their feet and cut the foamy trail that always disappears behind them. And after all the exploring of the world's many shorelines, Hawai'i continues to be the global headquarters for this ancient sport and pastime.

This was the first book to chart surfing's Pacific origins in the context of Polynesian culture. Its main outline was conceived and developed by Ben Finney as his master's thesis in anthropology at the University of Hawai'i. Much of the material was revised by James D. Houston, who also added new details and interpretations. For this thirtieth-anniversary edition, a number of seldom-seen drawings and early photos have been added, along with appendixes of vintage writings on the subject, from the unedited log of Captain Cook's second-in-command, Lt. James King, to Jack London's lively account of "A Royal Sport," which first appeared in 1907. A few historical and cultural details have been updated (e.g., pronunciation marks for Hawaiian terms and the use of

Polynesian place names, such as Rapa Nui and Aotearoa in lieu of Easter Island and New Zealand), but beyond these, we have decided not to expand the original text. We hope it can be read as a detailed history as well as a view of this sport at a particular moment in its evolution. Thus, our description of catching a wave (pages 16–19) predates the "Short Board" and the invention of the ankle-leash. And our account of surfing's decline on the outer Hawaiian Islands predates the rediscovery of famous breaks on Maui, Hawai'i, and elsewhere as the sport continued to spread outward from Waikīkī.

In the mid 1960s surfing in Tahiti seemed a forgotten skill. But then surfers from Australia, California, and Hawai'i began bringing their boards to Tahiti to surf, intriguing young Tahitians. Some say that the first of them to try modern surfing got their start by buying boards from Australians who needed the money to fly back home. By the 1980s young Polynesians were surfing all around Tahiti and the neighboring islands, and a Tahitian had won the French national surfing championships. Similarly, interest in modern surfing among the indigenous Māori people of Aotearoa exploded with the introduction in the early 1970s of foam and fiberglass boards, which could be cheaply and easily made locally. Māori youth living along the west and east coasts of the North Island took to the waves in great numbers, and since then many have achieved recognition in national and international competition.

As for the early spread from Hawai'i toward other shores, it dates back a bit farther than we were aware of when we first researched this book. Though George Freeth, who visited Redondo Beach in 1907, still stands as the sport's first popular ambassador, recent research has uncovered the fact that Hawaiians surfed the shores of Monterey Bay as long ago as 1885.

A trio of Hawaiian princes, nephews of King Kalākaua, were enrolled at a military school south of San Francisco. They sometimes spent weekends with a family friend in Santa Cruz, Mrs. Lyman Swan, whose mother was Hawaiian. On July 20, 1885, the following item appeared in a local paper, *The Santa Cruz Daily Surf*, in a column called "Beach Breezes":

> The young Hawaiian princes were in the water enjoying it immensely and giving interesting exhibitions of surfboard swimming as practiced in their native land.

This is the first recorded instance of board-surfing on the West Coast, though not the first word of wave-riding there. That is to be found in Richard Henry Dana's *Two Years Before the Mast* (Boston, 1840). Dana was a New Englander who had left Harvard for medical reasons and went to sea on a trading ship bound for California, by way of Cape Horn, in search of cattle hides. The ship's first West Coast stop was Santa Barbara. It was January 1835. Young Dana was in the first long-boat trying to make the beach, and a heavy winter swell was running. The Americans were worried about capsizing in the shorebreak, when they were shown how to maneuver by a crew from another merchant ship that had recently dropped anchor. These were Hawaiian sailors accustomed to moving canoes through rushing surf:

> The sun had just gone down; it was getting dusky; the damp night wind was beginning to blow, and the heavy swell of the Pacific was setting in, and breaking loud and high "combers" on the beach. We lay on our oars in the swell, just outside the surf, waiting for a good chance to run it, when a boat which had put off from the Ayacucho just after us came alongside of us, with a crew of dusky Sandwich Islanders talking and hallooing in their outlandish tongue.

They knew that we were novices in this kind of boating, and waited to see us go in. The second mate, however, who steered our boat, determined to have the advantage of their experience and would not go in first. Finding at length how matters stood, they gave a shout and taking advantage of a great comber which came swelling in rearing its head . . . they gave three or four long and strong pulls, and went in on top of the great wave, throwing their oars overboard, as far from the boat as they could throw them, and jumping out the instant that the boat touched the beach, and then seizing hold of her and running her high and dry upon the sand.

The watermen who rode to shore that evening in 1835 had learned their wave-sliding skills in an archipelago that lay some 2,500 miles farther west. Where they came from, intimacy with every nuance of the all-surrounding sea was part of daily life; it was part of a cultural legacy already many centuries old, and tied to a mid-Pacific world so remote that, in those days, very few people outside Hawai'i had any idea where it was. Geographically, it is still the most isolated place on Earth, the farthest removed from another land mass. In order to find Hawai'i, ancestor-navigators long ago mastered trans-Pacific voyaging. How Hawaiians mastered the surf that fringes their home islands is still a story unique in the history of ocean-going peoples.

—B. F. and J.D.H.

Honolulu and Santa Cruz, 1996

Pronouncing Hawaiian

Until recently Hawaiian was written with seven consonants—h, l, m, n, p, k, and w—five vowels—a, e, i, o, u—and no diacritical marks. Now it is becoming common to employ two diacritical marks: the *ʻōkina* (ʻ) or glottal stop and the *kahakō* or macron (¯). The ʻokina actually represents a consonant. Its pronunciation is similar to the sound between the "ohs" in the English phrase "oh-oh." The ʻokina usually shows up between two vowels (as in *Hawaiʻi*), but it is the first character of some words, including ʻokina. The kahakō placed over vowels indicates stress or increased duration. These marks are necessary to correctly understand and pronounce written Hawaiian. Consider, for example, how the placement of the kahakō changes meaning: *pāʻu* refers to the long skirt worn by women horseback riders, while *paʻū* means soaked or drenched. Remove the kahakō and you've got *paʻu*, or soot. Then take out the ʻokina as well, and you're left with the familiar local monosyllable for finished: *pau*. For accuracy and to honor the unique language and culture of Hawaiʻi, we have tried to use the ʻokina and kahakō correctly throughout this book, following the usage in the *Hawaiian Dictionary*, by Mary Kawena Pukui and Samuel H. Elbert (University of Hawaiʻi Press, 1986), and in other authoritative works.

White-capped waves, billowy waves,

Waves that break into a heap,

    waves that break and spread.

The surf rises above them all,

The rough surf of the island,

The Great surf that pounds and thrashes,

The foamy surf of Hikiau.

It is the sea on which to surf at noon,

The sea that washes the pebbles and

    corals ashore.

      —from *The Surf Chant of Naihe,*
        Chief of Kaʻū *(translated by Mary Kawena Pukui)*

THIS IS THE FIRST KNOWN ENGRAVING OF A MAN ON A SURFBOARD, MADE FROM A SKETCH DRAWN IN 1778 DURING CAPTAIN COOK'S THIRD VOYAGE TO THE PACIFIC. THE FIGURE PADDLING AT LOWER LEFT IS HEADING OUT WITH OTHER HAWAIIANS TO MEET COOK'S SHIPS AT KEALAKEKUA BAY.

CHAPTER ONE

The Wave, the Board, and the Surfer

Here waves climb into dusk on gleaming mail;
Invisible valves of the sea, —locks, tendons
Crested and creeping, troughing corridors
That fall back yawning to another plunge.

—HART CRANE

Hawai'i's gift to the world of sport is surfing—sliding down the slope of a breaking wave on a surfboard. Long before Captain Cook sailed into Kealakekua Bay, Hawaiians had mastered the art of standing erect while speeding toward shore. Riding prone on a wave with the aid of a short bodyboard was practiced throughout the Pacific Islands, primarily by youngsters, and probably dates back thousands of years. The Hawaiians took this ancestral habit, lengthened the boards, refined their shapes, and developed techniques that moved Lt. James King, in the first published account of surfing, to exclaim, "The boldness and address with which I saw them perform these difficult and dangerous manoeuvers was altogether astonishing and is scarcely to be believed."[1]

Today this exhilarating sport is still Hawai'i's "national pastime." Hundreds of surfers daily accept the challenge of the islands' famous shorelines. Moreover, from Hawai'i the sport has spread to five continents and many more islands scattered among the world's oceans. Yet Hawai'i continues to be surfing's mecca, attracting surfers from around the world who come to test their skills on the giant winter swells generated by North Pacific storms or to enjoy the gentler waves that radiate up from the South Pacific each summer.

This book tells the history of surfing from its ancient Polynesian beginnings to its status as an international sport. It is a story full of myth and daring, courtship and craftsmanship, religion and ingenuity. Its details come from such sources as Hawaiian chants, explorers' journals, and manuscripts penned by newly literate Hawaiians, as well as from the testimony of the men and women who keep the sport alive today. The early sources tell how the sport was bound up with the traditional religion, sexual practices, and the system of social classes. Surfing feats and romantic encounters in the surf were celebrated in song and legend. Board builders followed sacred rituals, and at least one temple was solely dedicated to surfing. The privileged chiefs as well as people from all levels of society took part, and they achieved a proficiency in the water that has only recently been matched.

Later sources tell of the near death of the sport, its revival, and its current spread and development. Soon after the arrival of alien explorers, traders, and missionaries—and all the ills and opportunities they brought—surfing began to decline. For nearly a hundred years it was dying a slow death like so many other activities that had been woven into the religious and cultural fabric of Hawaiian civilization.

But surfing did not die out completely; at the beginning of this century it began to recover. The story of its renaissance is unique, since surfing today is one of the few features of traditional Hawaiian culture to reach out and establish itself in other parts of the world.

Before recounting this history, however, we need to know something about the sport itself. What is surfing? Where does it occur? What is the natural force that can send a surfer and a board streaking along the ocean's edge?

THE WAVE

The first requirement is a ridable wave. Surfing doesn't begin when surfers dip their arms into the water to paddle out to an approaching swell. It begins much earlier, far out at sea, typically hundreds or often thousands of miles from where the wave finally peaks and cracks to roll shoreward.

The primary wave-building force is wind, as it strikes the ocean's surface. Without wind we would have no waves. Waves formed by wind and ocean storms grow into irregular patterns called *seas*. Long periods of wind over wide ocean stretches produce heavy seas, and waves leaving these storm areas are called *swells*. They fan out much like ripples around a pebble dropped in a pond. They decrease in height, increase in length, and eventually become a series of long, low, and regular undulations called *ground swells.* Although these swells move through the ocean, very little water is displaced. Just as wind agitating a grainfield makes waves while the grain itself stays rooted in the earth, so the wave-*form* rolls through water, whereas the water molecules themselves move a little, but barely advance.

Swells usually travel in *sets* of from three to as many as twelve or so. The distance between the crests of two successive swells is called the wave *length*. As these swells enter shallow coastal waters of is-

lands or continents, ridable waves begin to form. When the water depth is one-half the wave length, the incoming swell begins to feel drag from the bottom. The distance between crests decreases. The swell slows down, and internal flow patterns cause the water to pile up as the wave back overtakes the wave front. Tons of water bulge from the ocean's surface.

A wave usually breaks when water depth equals one and one-third the wave's height. A six-foot wave, for example, will break in eight feet of water. A small wave will break closer to shore than a large one. Depending upon its size, then, and the shape of the bottom, an incoming swell will grow steeper and steeper until the crest rises sharply, peaks, and finally breaks in the roaring conclusion called *surf.*

A wave breaks in one of two main ways: either it *plunges* or it *spills*. The spiller, generally easier to ride, is caused by a relatively flat bottom. As a swell approaches the shallow water, its crest sharpens, crumbles into foam, and spills down the wave face. If well suited for surfing, it will not spill over all at once; rather, one section—the section moving through the shallowest water—will break first, and the spilling white water will spread from there across the wave as it rolls to shore, until the entire wave is white water. Such a wave is ideal because the surfer's objective is to slide diagonally across a wave's face, keeping ahead of the breaking foam. Thus, spillers usually provide longer rides.

Plungers are noisier and more spectacular. They are usually caused by a steeply sloping bottom. The swell rises quickly, until part of its face is vertical. Then the crest leaps out and pours into the wave's trough, forming for an instant a water tunnel. Turbulence makes a plunger more hazardous than a spiller, but when mastered it offers more excitement for the experienced surfer be-

HONOLULU ADVERTISER ©
1925

SURFERS TAKING OFF ON A WAVE AT WAIKĪKĪ, 1925. PHOTO FROM THE *HONOLULU ADVERTISER*, COURTESY BISHOP MUSEUM, HONOLULU.

cause of increased speed, steepness, and greater risks.

Whether a wave spills or plunges depends upon the shape of the ocean bottom. The wide variation in offshore topography provides unlimited possibilities in these two basic breaker types. Sand, coral reef, or a submerged rock formation will each produce its distinctive wave. A sandy beach, for example, may produce spillers in the winter and plungers in the summer, as storms and tidal power shift sand around to make the bottom flat or steeply sloped. The shape of a rocky headland, on the other hand, will rarely change, and any variation in the surf that breaks there will depend on the size and direction of the swell itself.

From wherever they come and however they break, most surfing waves, after traveling so far over the ocean, will have from fifteen to forty-five seconds to thunder and sizzle before they bury themselves in the ocean again and disappear in a million rolling bubbles. But while a surfable wave lasts, it offers its blue, inviting slope, and just behind the spot where it breaks, the surfer waits to catch a ride.

THE BOARD

Once the wave peaks there are three basic ways to ride it: in a canoe, by body-surfing, or on a board. For canoe-surfing, Hawaiians use an outrigger canoe, which because of its bulk needs a gently sloping wave. The entire crew paddles to catch an approaching swell. Once riding, the canoe moves slower than a board; the big craft skims ahead of the break but cannot angle as sharply. Its position is controlled by a paddle used over the stern as rudder. Body-surfers swim to catch a wave. Once part of it, they angle their bodies and head away from the break, bringing their arms to their sides and hunching their shoulders so that their upper bodies become the plan-

ing surface. The full-sized surfboard, however, with its capability for greater speed, larger waves, and a variety of maneuvers, has always been the most popular and dramatic means of riding.

Since early surfing times the board has developed almost as remarkably as the sport itself. Lieutenant King described the Hawaiians riding on "a long narrow board, rounded at the ends." The old cigar-shaped boards were carved from solid woods natural to Hawai'i and could weigh 150 pounds or more. At present [1966] a typical surfboard is made of molded plastic foam or balsa wood. It may weigh twenty-five pounds, but the weight varies according to the weight of the surfer and the type of wave the board will ride. It might be ten feet long, about two feet wide, and three inches deep, pointed at the nose with rounded edges, and tapering to a foot-wide flat tail. The whole board is covered with several layers of waterproofing, reinforcing fiberglass. The deck is flat, and the surfer usually waxes it with paraffin for surefootedness. The bottom is slightly rounded to allow smoother gliding, and a skeg, or tail-fin, serves as a kind of rudder to hold the board in the wave and facilitate turning. (The development of surfboard construction and performance is covered in greater detail in Chapter Five.)

THE SURFER

With a wave to ride and board to stand on, a surfer today enjoys the swells in much the same way as did the Hawaiians of old. The most arduous part, of course, is paddling through rushing surf to the take-off point. What follows here are the basics of surfing, in case you have not yet tested the waters yourself.

The ideal place to catch a wave is where its face is steepest and just about to break, so paddle out to a position just beyond the point where this will occur, and wait for a set to build. When a good wave

SURFERS ENJOYING A SMALL WAVE AT WAIKĪKĪ, C. 1910. PHOTO COURTESY HAWAI'I STATE ARCHIVES, HONOLULU.

humps up to cover the horizon, point your board toward the shore and, to gain speed, dig your arms in and start paddling. When your board is moving fast enough on the swell, the building wave's power will suddenly take hold, and you will accelerate as your board begins sliding freely down the slope. Then jump to your feet, turning the board to slide diagonally across the wall of water to keep in front of its toppling crest.

Riding "straight off" in front of the bounding white water is the more amateurish and sometimes more dangerous style, especially in big surf where the foam itself may form a tumbling wall six feet high. It is much more exhilarating to angle your board to the right and left and cross the wave's as-yet-unbroken face with the white water leaping and roaring behind you. The resultant speed is a combination of the wave's forward motion and your board's "across" motion. You are then skimming down a bottomless incline that continues building below you as it carries you shoreward.

Once you are standing and sliding diagonally across a wave, success depends upon your grace and balance and your ability to judge when and where the wave will break. If you slide too far out on the shoulder, your speed drops off, and if you stay too near the toppling crest it can overwhelm you. Standing too far forward on your board will make the nose dig in or "pearl dive," dumping you in the ocean. Neither can you stand too far back toward the tail, or your board rears up, loses its grip, and stalls. Stalling, however, can work to your advantage when you want to slow down until the break catches up with you, or to turn back into the faster part of the wave.

You control your ledgelike position on the wave with foot movements and shifts in body weight. By simultaneously leaning back on your rear foot and toward the direction you want to turn, you can bank your board to the right or left. Near shore you can turn your board into the break and ride the "soup" to the beach, or whip your board up and over the wave top and then paddle back to the take-off point. If a wave breaks right on you, you can try to ride it out, either standing or prone—or jump off the board, grab the nose, and push it under the wave to get clear of it on the seaward side. If you fall off or are knocked off, your board heads toward the beach with the wave while you have to swim for it.

After an inevitable period of awkwardness while learning, the aspiring surfer acquires the necessary skills, finds just the right board, and knows how to recognize some good waves. These three elements produce the experience called surfing.

Only one other factor remains to be explained: the actual physics of the sport. What is it that propels the board across this moving slope? From a surfer's viewpoint several forces are involved: the buoyancy of the board itself; the surfer's initial speed-building paddle, which overcomes friction between the board and the water; the take-off and drop, when gravity pulls the board downward as the ride begins; and the push a moving wave imparts to the board. A precise description of the relationship between these forces is the job of the marine physicist. Let us be content with an amateur's theory on "the physics of surfing" offered by Jack London in 1907 after he tried to master the sport during a visit to Hawai'i on his yacht, *The Snark*:

> Lie out there quietly on your board. Sea after sea breaks before, behind and under and over you, and rushes in on shore, leaving you behind. When a wave crests, it gets steeper. Imagine yourself, on your board, on the face of that steep slope. If it stood still, you would slide down just as a boy slides down a hill on a coaster. "But," you object, "the wave doesn't stand still." Very true, but the water composing the wave stands still, and there you have the secret. If you ever start sliding down the face of that wave, you'll keep on sliding and you'll never reach the bottom. Please don't laugh. The face may be six feet, yet you can slide down it a quarter of a mile, or half a mile, and not reach the bottom. For, see, since a wave is only communicated agitation or impetus, and since the water that composes the wave is changing every instant, new water is rising into the wave as fast as the wave travels. You slide down this new water and yet remain in your old position on the

wave skidding down the still newer water that is rising and forming the wave . . . between you and the shore stretches a quarter mile of water. As the wave travels, this water obligingly heaps itself into the wave, gravity does the rest, and down you go sliding the whole length of it. . . .

And now for another phase of the physics of surf-riding. All rules have their exceptions. It is true that the water in the wave does not travel forward. But there is what may be called the send of the sea. The water in the overtoppling crest does move forward, as you will speedily realize if you are slapped in the face by it, or if you are caught under it and are pounded by one mighty blow down under the surface panting and gasping for a half a minute. The water in the top of the wave rests upon the water in the bottom of the wave. But when the bottom of the wave strikes land, it stops, while the top goes on. . . . Where was solid water beneath it, is now air, and for the first time it feels the grip of gravity, and down it falls, at the same time being torn asunder from the lagging bottom of the wave and flung forward. And it is because of this that riding a surfboard is something more than mere placid sliding down a hill. In truth, one is caught up and hurled shoreward as by some Titan's hand.[2]

Good surfing waves are not unusual; they occur frequently in many parts of the world. The sport depends on more than waves, however. Before the advent of protective wet suits, no one surfed the more northerly beaches bathed in frigid water. Relatively warm water and a climate favorable for outdoor sports are necessary, as are people without fear of the sea. All these conditions exist in varying degrees on most of the islands of the open Pacific and in several other areas around the globe. Indeed, surfing's global spread has depended on this. Yet in all of the Pacific—and throughout the world, for that matter—the islands of Hawai'i are probably the best adapted for riding ocean waves.

The whole archipelago, well within the tropic zone, is blessed with a general coastal water temperature of 70 degrees or more. Although coral reefs edge most of the islands, they do not absorb the ocean swell before it hits shore. In the best surfing areas these reefs combine with sandy or rocky bottoms to shape swells ideal for surfing, at distances from twenty-five yards to a quarter mile from shore. Hawai'i is fortunately located, moreover, because it is in the path of the Pacific's dominant swells. O'ahu, the island best suited to surfing, receives ground swells from both the North and South Pacific. It catches the "north swell" from October through January as it rolls away from winter storms near Siberia and Alaska. During the summer, from May to October, O'ahu's southern shore takes the "south swell" from storm centers as far away as the high latitudes of the South Pacific.

Surfing in Hawai'i is a year-round sport in water and weather that is perpetually warm. Because of the variety of swells the islands receive and the variety of shoreline and bottom combinations—long sand beaches, coral reefs, jutting lava headlands, lagoons, and curving bays—there is surf to suit every level of riding skill. For beginners, there are the usually gentle rollers at Waikīkī; for the "pros," the terrifying, twenty-five foot giants of Mākaha and Sunset Beach—waves that can snap a board like a twig or catch a tiny rip in its fiberglass cover and flay it clean. It isn't surprising then when we find that Hawai'i is still surfing's capital and that in ancient times the sport developed there to a degree far in advance of any other island group in the Pacific.

Early Hawaiian surfers, 1874. Engraving by Emile Bayard.

CHAPTER TWO

Pacific Origins

The tide of emigration, let it roll
as it will, never overwhelms the
backwoodsman unto itself; he rides
upon the advance, as the Polynesian
upon the comb of the surf.

—HERMAN MELVILLE

The Pacific Ocean isn't always true to its name. It generates raging storms and produces some of the largest sea swells in the world. For ages its waves have pounded the shores of continents and islands, heaping an obstacle between humanity and the open sea, warning us of what crushing power the ocean holds. In several parts of the Pacific, however, the island people turned the restless edges of this ocean to their own advantage. In search of recreation, they learned to ride the waves. Surrounded by the sounds and spectacle of the sea, they were the first to tame its less-violent offerings.

No one knows who first realized the possibilities of riding the swells that had always been so much a part of island life. It may have been a weary swimmer, bounced all the way to the beach in a white boil, or a fisherman in a canoe, straining to make shore in heavy seas, or simply a youngster playing in the waves who first knew the thrill of racing across the rising slopes. Simple board-surfing—in which a swimmer uses a short plank or other aid to ride a wave just for the fun of it—was practiced throughout the Pacific Islands. Recreational wave-riding was probably part of the general marine adaptation pioneered by the first people to enter the open Pacific. That would date the beginnings of the sport back to almost 2000 B.C., when the ances-

tors of the Polynesians and other Pacific islanders started moving eastward from Southeast Asia to explore and colonize this vast oceanic region. Recent archaeological finds suggest that the first canoes reached Hawai'i by at least A.D. 400. Those first settlers were probably already skilled in simple surfing, and perhaps after several hundred years of riding Hawai'i's big waves they began to develop the big boards, the art of standing up while riding diagonally across a wave front, and other features of this uniquely Hawaiian form of the sport. A cautious guess would then date Hawaiian surfing back at least a thousand years.

If the earliest dates are vague, there is no doubt that by the eighteenth century Hawaiians had been surfing long enough to develop skills that amazed European explorers and other early visitors. Among those who left us the first written descriptions of what they called "wave-riding," "surf-riding," or "surf-boarding" was Lieutenant King, whose surprise upon witnessing how the Hawaiians rode the waves we have already noted in Chapter One. He went on to say, "Their first object is to place themselves on the summit of the largest surge, by which they are driven with amazing rapidity towards shore."

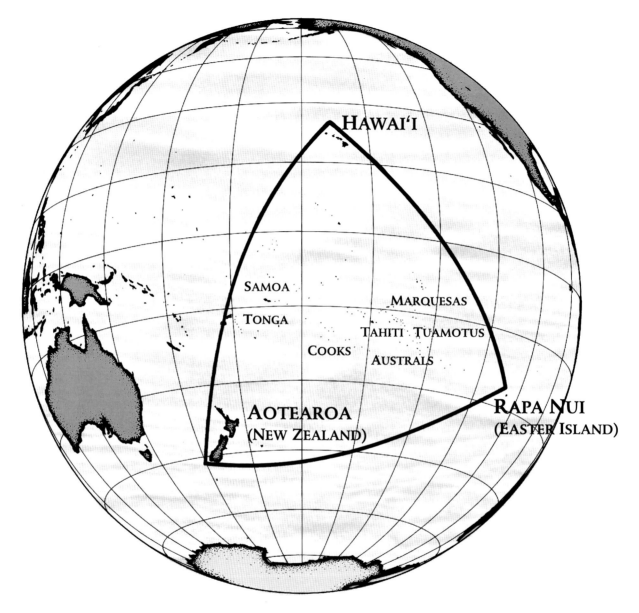

FIGURE 1.

INDIGENOUS BOARD-SURFING IN THE PACIFIC WAS MOST HIGHLY DEVELOPED ON ISLANDS WITHIN THE POLYNESIAN TRIANGLE BOUNDED BY HAWAI'I, RAPA NUI (EASTER ISLAND), AND AOTEAROA (NEW ZEALAND). EARLY REPORTS OF SURFING ALONG THE SHORES OF ISLANDS FROM NEW GUINEA TO POLYNESIA INDICATE THAT THIS SPORT, AT LEAST IN ITS RUDIMENTARY FORM, WAS PART OF THE COMMON HERITAGE OF THE SEAFARING PEOPLE WHO SPREAD ACROSS THE PACIFIC THOUSANDS OF YEARS AGO.

Hawaiians, of course, were not alone in their enjoyment of the Pacific's waves. A few years later and two thousand plus miles south, James Morrison, boatswain's mate on the HMS *Bounty*, observed how Tahitians reveled in riding the surf. Other early accounts establish that surfing was enjoyed throughout Polynesia, that great triangle of islands bounded by Hawai'i in the north, lonely Rapa Nui (the indigenous name for Easter Island) in the southeast, and the massive islands of Aotearoa (New Zealand) in the southwest. But the sport, at least in its most rudimentary form, was not purely Polynesian. As indicated in figure 1, some form of surfing with a board—or with the stem of a coconut frond, a bundle of reeds, or just about anything that would provide a little buoyancy and a planing surface—was practiced throughout the Pacific islands. Yet there was a great difference between Hawaiian surfing and surfing elsewhere in the Pacific that becomes apparent when we consider who surfed, the size of the boards, and how the boards were ridden.

The first point, the surfers themselves, is important because it suggests the sport's social position. Who were the people who took part in a sport that embraced hundreds of Pacific Islands? Were they adults or children, men or women, chiefs or commoners? On the islands of the western Pacific and along the western edge of Polynesia, surfing was mainly a children's pastime, dominated by boys, if we can trust the accounts. By contrast, on most main islands of East Polynesia* surfing was a sport for both sexes and all ages. For example, in Tahiti, the *Bounty*'s Morrison wrote, "at this diversion all sexes were excellent . . . the children also take their sport in the smaller surfs."[1] The same seems to have been the case for the Māori people of Aotearoa and for the surfers of Marquesas and Rapa, located to the

TAHITIAN BOY SURFING ON A BODYBOARD, MID 1950S.
PHOTO COURTESY BUD BROWNE.

northeast and south of Tahiti, respectively. Above all, in Hawai'i everyone enjoyed the sport, men and women, young and old. And as we shall see in the next chapter, the chiefs of Hawai'i were especially adept at surfing.

The other points of comparison—board size and riding position—are closely related, since a board's shape and length determine how one rides it. Two basic board types are used in the surf. A bodyboard (also known as a belly board or a *paipo* board) is usually from two to four feet long and is used as an auxiliary aid in sliding across a wave. Surfers using bodyboards actually swim, holding the boards in front of themselves as planing surfaces. This is commonly a children's pas-

---

*Primarily Hawai'i, the Marquesas Islands, Tahiti and the surrounding Society Islands, the Cook Islands, plus Aotearoa. Although Aotearoa forms the southwestern corner of Polynesia, it is classified culturally as East Polynesian because it was probably settled from the Cooks and the Societies.

time. True surfing requires a full-sized board, usually six feet or longer and at least around eighteen inches wide, that can support the rider entirely, allowing him or her to ride prone, kneeling or standing. Early accounts specifically mention long boards in only two island groups: Hawai'i and Aotearoa. Aotearoa boards are described as reaching six feet in length, but because they were only some nine inches wide they probably did not allow a rider to stand up. Morrison says boards of "any length" were used in Tahiti and that the more expert Tahitians could stand up while surfing, which implies that some of the Tahitian boards were approaching surfboard size. The next largest boards in Polynesia—four-foot planks in the Marquesas and long reed bundles from Rapa Nui (where because of deforestation there was little wood available)—apparently did not allow the riders to stand up. Elsewhere in Polynesia and the rest of the Pacific island region the boards were short bodyboards, and there is no mention of riders sitting, kneeling, or standing erect.

THIS LATE 1800S PRINT SHOWS HAWAIIAN SURFERS STANDING, PRONE, AND SITTING ON WAVES.
PHOTO COURTESY HAWAI'I MARITIME CENTER, HONOLULU.

The Hawaiians, however, possessed true surfboards. The largest of these were eighteen or more feet long, two feet wide, and five or six inches thick, and could weigh 150 pounds or more. Such boards are still preserved in Honolulu's museums. They were buoyant enough to support the rider and allow all the riding positions: prone, sitting, kneeling, and standing. It is well known that Hawaiians were capable of all these maneuvers in the surf around their islands. This variety of skills, on long boards, together with the widespread participation of all classes was unequaled in any other Pacific island group.

Tahitian surfers came the closest. Although board lengths are not definitely established, we know that Tahitians sometimes rode in a kneeling position. And according to Morrison, some eighteenth-century experts could stand on their boards, at least momentarily. That both men and women and particularly the chiefs of Tahiti enjoyed the sport suggests its high development there. It is doubtful, however, that Tahiti's chiefs could have won a surfing contest at Waikīkī. One of the few men who observed the sport in both groups during the nineteenth century, William Ellis, made this observation of the Tahitian surfers:

> Their surf-boards are inferior to those of the Sandwich Islanders [Hawaiians], and I do not think swimming in the sea as an amusement, whatever it might have been formerly, is now practiced so much by the natives of the South, as by those of the North.[2]

It is tempting to consider that the Hawaiian and Tahitian developments were not just parallel but were actually connected. Many legends describe canoe voyages between Tahiti and Hawai'i made some seven or eight centuries ago, reckoned by counting back the generations in the chiefly genealogies in which the heroic voyagers appear. One legend tells of a chief who sailed from Tahiti to Hawai'i and then abandoned his voyaging life to "live and die" near a famous surfing break on Kaua'i. These tales, plus the apparent incorporation of Tahitian features in the language of the Hawaiians and their material culture and social structure, suggest that the two cultures may have been in contact around A.D. 1200. The high degree of surfing development in both places may therefore be an example of cultural sharing dating from this period, although we can only speculate over whether Tahitian or Hawaiian surfers took the first steps in developing the sport beyond a children's pastime.

Was board-surfing limited to the Pacific islands? In all the world, we have found only two other places where surfing may have developed independently from the Pacific island sport: West Africa and northern Peru. From Senegal, Ivory Coast, and Ghana come reports of bodyboard surfing, which, particularly since they date back to the 1830s, may indicate that African youths along this coast independently hit upon the idea of using planks to ride the waves. From northern Peru there are descriptions of fishermen who fish offshore sitting on reed bundles, which they call *caballitos* (little horses). When done fishing, they paddle back to shore (using a wooden paddle) and catch a wave or two coming in through the surf, a practice that may be of great antiquity since fishermen sitting astride and paddling their caballitos are featured in pre-Columbian pottery. However, in neither of these cases did surfing develop into anything like Hawaiian surfing. And these rudimentary forms do not seem to have spread elsewhere. Even though modern surfing now flourishes along the beaches of Peru and South Africa, it spread there from Hawai'i—as will be explained in our last chapter.

Although exact relationships between islands may be obscure, the following sequence in the origin of Hawaiian surfing seems likely. First, those early canoe voyagers—who initiated the exploration and colonization of the Pacific some four thousand years ago—developed rudimentary board-surfing: primarily a children's pastime practiced with short bodyboards. As their descendants pushed farther into the Pacific, they carried this pastime with them. Then, on some of the main islands of East Polynesia it came to be taken up more and more by adult men and women using larger boards. Finally, along the shores of the Hawaiian Islands, surfing reached its peak. There the feat of standing erect on a speeding board found its finest expression.

Early explorers found the "Hawaiian sport of surf playing" to be a national pastime.

CHAPTER THREE

Aliʻi, Olo, and Alaia

Arise! Arise, ye great surfs from Kahiki,
The powerful curling waves.
Arise with pōhuehue.
Well up, long raging surf.

With the Hawaiians' mastery of the sport itself, the story has barely begun. As a part of the fabled Hawaiian way of life of pre-European times, surfing was more than just catching and riding an ocean wave. It was the center of a circle of social and ritual activities that began with the very selection of the tree from which a board was carved and could end in the premature death of a chief—as was the result of at least one famous surfing contest in Hawaiian legend.

Early writers, observing its popularity and the obvious relish and sometimes passionate dedication with which Hawaiians approached the sport, referred to it as "a national pastime," "a most prominent and popular pastime," or "a favorite amusement." When the British ship *Blonde* stopped in Hawaiʻi in the early 1820s her commander, Lord Byron, cousin to the poet, noted, "to have a neat floatboard, well-kept, and dried, is to a Sandwich Islander what a tilbury or cabriolet, or whatever light carriage may be in fashion is to a young English man."[1]

In 1823 the missionary C. S. Stewart observed that on Maui the surfboard formed "an article of personal property among all the chiefs, male and female, and among many of the common people."[2] After a run of particularly heavy waves off the Lāhainā coast he added that such surf provided "a fine opportunity to the islanders for the enjoyment of their favorite sport of the surfboard. It is a daily amusement at all times, but the more terrific the surf, the more delightful the pastime to those skillful in the management of the boards. . . . hundreds at a time have been occupied in this way for hours together." And Ellis, that adventurous missionary who hiked around the island of Hawaiʻi, described the islanders' mass reaction to a sudden run of good waves: "the thatch houses of a whole village stood empty," he said; "daily tasks such as farming, fishing and tapa-making were left undone while an entire community—men, women and children—enjoyed themselves in the rising surf and rushing white water."

Such village-wide participation was never difficult to organize. Because of climate, their means of livelihood, and a general dependence on the ocean, most Hawaiians lived near the warm, balmy coasts. And the location of ancient surfing places coincides very closely with the location of these coastal settlements and with areas of population density. The maps of "Surfing Places in Ancient Hawaiʻi" [fig. 2–4] show a profusion along the Kona coast on the island of Hawaiʻi. When the first European explorers arrived, this particular coast was the major population center, not only for the Big Island but for the whole group. Together with the Waikīkī district of Oʻahu, it was also

SURFING PLACES OF ANCIENT HAWAII

Where did the Hawaiians surf in the old days? Many of the old names can be found in traditional songs, chants, and legends in which surfing contests, the wave-riding feats of champions, romantic encounters, and other events revolving around surfing at a particular place are mentioned. Also useful are the writings of such great nineteenth-century Hawaiian historians as John Papa I'i and Samuel Manaiakalani Kamakau. Although these sources usually give the specific name of the surfing break, sometimes they only mention the geographical region (usually a bay, point, or land section) where surfing was practiced. The lists and maps of surfing spots for each island below were developed from these sources, as well as from a welcome gift to the authors from Mary Kawena Pukui of a stack of file cards on which she had written the names of surfing places that she had run across during her decades of translating and interpreting Hawaiian oral traditions and newspaper articles from the nineteenth century. Where possible, we have listed each surfing spot according to its general location as well as the specific name of the break, italicizing the latter. Where we have only one name, be it of a break or a more general geographical locale, it also has been italicized. Following the authoritative works of Pukui, Elbert, and Mookini (1974) and Pukui and Elbert (1986) listed in the bibliography, we have hyphenated the names to indicate the words embodied in each and have given literal translations where available.

Figure 2.

HAWAI'I

1 Nā-'ohaku, *Kūmoho*, "to rise (as water)"
2 East of Kauhola Point, *Hale-lua*, "pit house"
3 *Wai-manu*, "bird water"
4 *Wai-pi'o*, "curved water"
5 *Lau-pāhoehoe*, "smooth lava flat"
6 *Pāpa'i-kou*, "hut [in a] kou [grove]"
7 *Kapo'ai*, "to rotate or revolve" (as in a hula)
8 Pu'u'eo, *Pā-'ula*, "red enclosure"
9 Hilo Bay
    a *Āhua*, "heap'
    b *Huia*, "a type of high wave formed when two crests meet"
    c *Kai-palaoa*, "whale sea"
    d *Ka-hala-'ia*, "the sin of eating forbidden fish or meat"
    e *Kā-nuku-o-ka-manu* (near Waiākea), "the beak of the bird"
    f *Kāwili*, "to mix, blend, intertwine"
    g *Pi'ihonua*, "land incline"
10 Ke'eau, *Ka-loa-o-ka-'oma*, "the length of the oven"
11 Kai-mū, "gathering [at the] sea [to watch surfing]"
    a *Hō-'eu*, "mischief"
    b *Ka-poho*, "the depression"
12 Kala-pana
    a *Ā'ili*, "to struggle for breath, to pull"
    b *Ka-lehua*, "the expert"
13 Puna-lu'u, *Kāwā*, "distance"
14 Ka-'alu'alu Bay
    a *Pai-a-ha'a*, "lift and sway [of waves]"
    b *Kua'ana*, "big brother" (the outside surf for grown-ups)
    c *Kaina*, "little brother" (the inside surf for children)
15 East of Ka-lae (South Point), *Ka-pu'u-one*, "the sand hill"
16 *Ke'ei*

17 Nā-pō‘opo‘o

    a *Ka-pahu-kapu*, "the taboo drum"

    b *Kapukapu*, "regal appearance"

    c *Kukui*, "candlenut tree, torch"

18 Ke-ala-ke-kua, *Hiki-au*, "moving current" (opposite the *heiau* of the same name where Captain Cook was received as a personification of the god Lono)

19 Ke-au-hou (He‘eia Bay)

    a *Ka-lapu*, "the ghost"

    b *Kaulu*, "ledge"

20 Kaha-lu‘u

    a *Ka-lei-kini*, "the many leis"

    b *Kapu‘a*, "the whistle"

21 Ke-olo-nā-hihi

    a *Ka-moa*, "the chicken"

    b *Kāwā*, "distance"

    c *Pu‘u*, "peak"

22 Kai-lua

    a *‘Au-hau-kea-‘ē*

    b *Huihā* (opposite Kona Inn)

    c *Ka-maka-i‘a*, "the fish eye"

    d *Ki‘i-kau*, "placed image"

    e *Nā-‘ōhule-‘elua*, "the two bald heads"

23 *Honokāhau*, "bay tossing dew"

24 Mahai‘ula, *Ka-hale-‘ula*, "the red house"

25 Kawaihae, *Ka-pua-‘ilima*, "the ‘ilima flower"

26 Honoipu, *Pua-kea*, "white blossom"

NOT LOCATED:

27 Kohala, *Ho‘olana*, "to cause to float"

28 Puna

    a *‘Āwili*, "swirl"

    b *Ka-lālani*, "the row"

    c *Kala-loa*, "very rough"

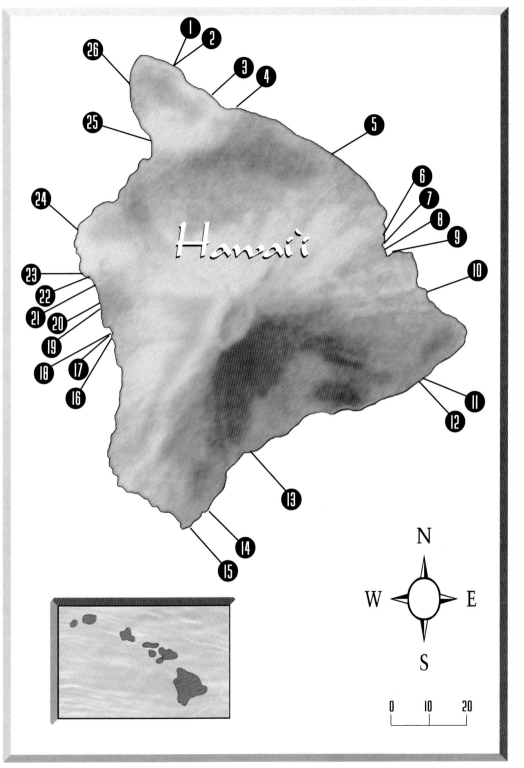

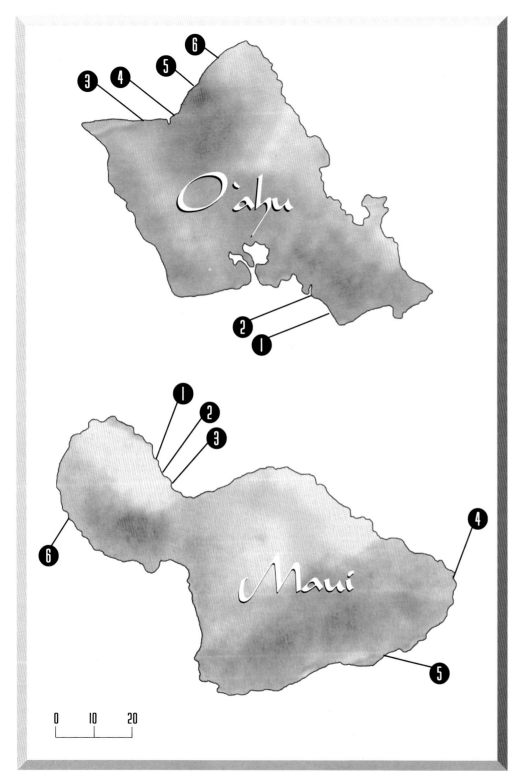

Figure 3.
Oʻahu and Maui

OʻAHU

1 Wai-kīkī (Although Waikīkī literally means "spouting water," it actually refers to the fresh water (*wai*) in the swamps behind the famous beach, not to the sea water (*kai*) of the surf offshore.)

    a *ʻAi-wohi*, "royal ruler"

    b *Ka-lehua-wehe*, "the removed *lehua* [lei]"

    c *Ka-pua*, "the flower"

    d *Ka-puni*, "the surrounding"

    e *Mai-hiwa*

2 Hono-lulu

    a *ʻUla-kua*, "back red"

    b *Ke-kai-o-Māmala*, "the sea of Māmala [a chiefess]"

    c *Awa-lua*, "double harbor"

3 Moku-lēʻia, *Pekue*

4 Wai-a-lua, *Pua-ʻena*, "issue hot"

5 Wai-mea River mouth, *Wai-mea*, "reddish water"

6 Pau-malū Bay, *Pau-malū*, "taken secretly" (now known as "Sunset Beach")

NOT LOCATED

7 Wai-a-lua

    a *Ka-pāpala*, "the crest"

    b *Ka-ua-nui*, "the big rain"

8 Wai-ʻanae

    a *Ka-pae-kahi*, "the single landing"

    b *Kuala-i-ka-pō-iki*, "tumbling in the small night"

9 *Ka-ʻihu-waʻa*, "the nose [of the] canoe"

MAUI

1 Wai-heʻe

    a *Ka-hāhā-wai*, "the broken rivulets"

    b *Pala-ʻie*, "inconstant"

    c *Pōpō-ʻie*, "ʻie vine cluster"

2 Wai-ehu

    a *ʻAʻawa*, "wrasse fish"

    b *Niu-kū-kahi*, "coconut palm standing alone"

3 Wai-luku

    a *Kaʻahu*, "the garment"

    b *Kaʻākau-pōhaku*, "the north (or right hand side) stone"

    c *Ka-leholeho*, "the callus"

    d *Paukū-kalo*, "taro piece"

4 Hana Bay

    a *Ke-ʻanini*, "the stunted"

    b *Pū-hele (Puʻu-hele)*, "traveling hill"

5 Kau-pō, *Moku-lau*, "many islets"

6 Lā-hainā

    a *ʻAʻaka*, "roiled"

    b *Hau-ola*, "dew [of] life"

    c *ʻŪhā-ʻī lio*, "dog's hindquarters"

    d *ʻUo*

NOT LOCATED

7 Hana (either bay or district), *Ka-puaʻi*, "the flow [of water]"

8 Lā-hainā

    a *Hale-lua*, "pit house"

    b *Ka-lehua*, "the expert"

Figure 4.
Kaua'i, Moloka'i, Ni'ihau, Lāna'i

KAUA'I

1 Anahola, *Ka-nahā-wale*, "easily broken"
2 Kapa'a
    a *Ka-maka-iwa*, "the mother-of-pearl eyes"
    b *Po'o*, "head"
    c *Ko'a-lua*, "two coral heads"
3 Wai-lua
    a *Maka-iwa*, "mother-of-pearl eyes"
    b *Ka-'ō-hala*, "the thrust passing"
4 *Hana-pēpē*, "crushed bay" (due to land slides)
5 Wai-mea
    a *Kaua*, "war"
    b *Kua-lua*, "twice"
    c *Po'o*, "head"

NOT LOCATED

6 Hana-lei District
    a *Hawai'i-loa*, "long (or distant) Hawai'i"
    b *Ho'ope'a*, "to cross"
    c *Kū-a-kahi-unu*, "standing like a fishing shrine"
    d *Makawa*
    e *Pu'u-lena*, "yellow hill"

7 Wai-'oli, *Mana-lau*, "many branches"

MOLOKA'I

1 Ka-laupapa, *Pua'ō*, "onslaught of dashing waves"

NI'IHAU

1 Ka-malino, *Lana*, "floating"
2 Pu'uwai, *'Ōhi'a*, "'ōhi'a tree"
3 *Ka-unu-nui*, "the large altar"

LĀNA'I

NOT LOCATED

1 *Hilole*

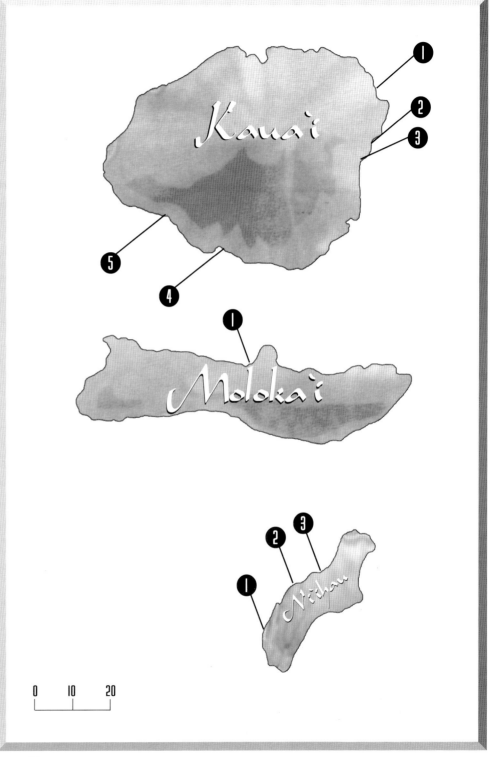

one of the most heavily surfed areas. It was along the Kona coast that Kamehameha I, the high chief who in the late 1790s and early 1800s united the islands into a single kingdom, learned to surf. And it was the surfing of the Hawaiians in Kona's Kealakekua Bay that so impressed Lieutenant King during his stay there in 1779 as an officer on Cook's expedition. Realizing the unique nature of the sport, King attempted to describe it in full:[3]

> Whenever, from stormy weather, or any extraordinary swell at sea, the impetuosity of the surf is increased to its utmost heights, they choose that time for their amusement, which is performed in the following manner: Twenty or thirty of the natives, taking each a long narrow board, rounded at the ends, set out together from the shore. The first wave they meet, they plunge under, and suffering it to roll over them, rise again beyond it, and make the best of their way, by swimming, out into the sea. The second wave is encountered in the same manner with the first. . . . As soon as they have gained by these repeated efforts, the smooth water beyond the surf, they lay themselves at length on their board, and prepare for their return. As the surf consists of a number of waves, of which every third is remarked to be always much larger than the others, and to flow higher on the shore, the rest breaking in the intermediate space, their first object is to place themselves on the summit of the largest surge. . . . If by mistake they should place themselves on one of the smaller waves, which breaks before they reach the land, or should not be able to keep their plank in a proper direction on the top of the swell, they are left exposed to the fury of the next, and, to avoid it, are obliged again to dive and regain their place, from which they set out. Those who succeed in their object of reaching shore, have still the greatest danger to encounter. The coast being guarded by a chain of rocks, with, here and there, a small opening between them, they are obliged to steer their boards through one of these, or, in case of failure, to quit it, before they reach the rocks, and, plunging under the wave, make the best of their way back again. This is reckoned very disgraceful, and is also attended with the loss of the board, which I have often seen, with great horror, dashed to pieces, at the very moment the islander quitted it.*

Hawaiian shores still provide such places where the sea and the land meet to produce excellent surfing waves. Today [1966] comparative handfuls are visited regularly by modern surfers. But in old Hawaiian stories and songs, dozens of surfing areas and often individual breaks have been remembered on every island in the group. Although a surfboard is now a rare sight on the once-popular Kona coastline, or anywhere on the Big Island for that matter, early sources have revealed some fifty individual surfing places on the island of Hawai'i alone. For the other six inhabited islands, fifty-eight more locations formerly used for surfing have been discovered: eighteen in O'ahu, nineteen on Maui, sixteen on Kaua'i, three on Ni'ihau, one on Moloka'i, and one on Lāna'i.

Among these were two well-known breaks, Kaulu and Kalapu at Keauhou, Kona, where King Kamehameha III surfed when he visited his birthplace. And on the northernmost island of Kaua'i broke the

---

* This is taken from the official publication on Cook's third voyage which was heavily edited by Reverend John Douglas. He had the habit of adding material of his own and from other accounts of the voyage. King's original words are printed in Beaglehole (1967, vol. 1, p. 268) and are reproduced as an appendix in this book.

famous curving surf of Makaiwa. According to legend, centuries ago when high-ranking Tahitians and Hawaiians were sailing back and forth between their respective islands, a chief named Moʻikeha ended his wandering days by settling on Kauaʻi "to live and die" near this famous surf. After a long sojourn in Tahiti, Moʻikeha had sailed north in his double-hulled canoe to the island of Hawaiʻi and then island-hopped along the chain until he came to Kauaʻi, the northernmost inhabited island. When Moʻikeha and his companions came ashore at Wailua Bay, a big surf was running and the people were gathering to ride the swells of Makaiwa just offshore. Moʻikeha joined them in their sport, and while enjoying the waves, the handsome stranger was spied by two sisters, Hoʻoipokamalani and Hinauʻu, who just happened to be the daughters of the ruling chief of Kauaʻi. Moʻikeha in turn was taken by their beauty and soon thereafter married both of them. Later, upon the death of his father-in-law, he became the ruling chief of the island. As Moʻikeha neared the end of his life, he longed to see once more his Tahitian son Laʻa, and so he sent his Kauaʻi-born son Kila to Tahiti to fetch Laʻa. After a long sail and many adventures, Kila finally reached Tahiti. Upon identifying himself as a son of Moʻikeha, he was asked by the Tahitians about the fate of his father and is said to have replied with these words:

I walea i Kauaʻi

I ka lā hiki aʻe a pō iho,

I keʻekeʻe a ka nalu o Makaiwa,

I kāhuli mai a ka pua kukui o Puna,

O ka waihalau o Wailua,

Noho no iā Kauaʻi a make iā Kauaʻi.

He is dwelling in ease in Kauaʻi

Where the sun rises and sets,

Where the surf of Makaiwa curves and bends,

Where the kukui blossoms of Puna change,

Where the waters of Wailua stretch out,

He will live and die on Kauaʻi.[4]

Another well-known surf called Kalehuawehe breaks at Waikīkī, the famous surfing spot on Oʻahu's southern shore. Here a few times a year huge swells march up from the south to provide a moving wave front that can sometimes be taken all the way to the beach. A ride on a twenty-to-thirty-foot wave from Kalehuawehe—or "Outside Castles," as it became known in the 1920s and 1930s—was considered the ultimate experience by the surfers of that era. According to legend the name Ka-lehua-wehe (the removed lehua) was inspired by a surfer who while riding at this break removed his lei made from lehua blossoms and presented it to a chiefess who was also riding there.

Several miles down the coast past Waikīkī there was a break called Ke-kai-o-Māmala (The Sea of Māmala). It broke through a narrow entrance to what is now Honolulu harbor straight out from a beautiful coconut grove called Honokaʻupu and provided some of the finest waves in Kou (an early name for the Honolulu area). The break was named after Māmala, a famous surfer and a prominent Oʻahu chiefess. She was a kupua, a demigod or hero with supernatural powers who could take the form of a beautiful woman, a gigantic lizard, or a great shark. According to legend, she was first married to another kupua, the shark-man Ouha; but then Honokaʻupu, who owned the coconut

MASKED PADDLERS ON A DOUBLE-HULLED CANOE. ENGRAVING FROM COOK'S *VOYAGE TO THE PACIFIC OCEAN* (1784).

grove, chose her to be his wife, and so Māmala left Ouha. Angered by this and ridiculed by women in his attempts to regain his wife, Ouha cast off his human form and became the great shark god of the coast between Waikīkī and Koko Head. The beautiful Māmala was remembered afterward in the surfing place named for her and in a song about her triangular love affair called the *Mele* (song) *of Honoka'upu*:

> The surf rises at Ko'olau,
>
> Blowing the waves into mist,
>
> Into little drops,
>
> Spray falling along the hidden harbor.
>
> There is my dear husband Ouha,
>
> There is the shaking sea, the running sea of Kou,
>
> The crab-like sea of Kou. . . .
>
> My love has gone away. . . .
>
> Fine is the breeze from the mountain.
>
> I wait for you to return, . . .
>
> Will the lover [Ouha] return?
>
> I belong to Honoka'upu,
>
> From the top of the tossing surf waves. . . .[5]

On the north shore of O'ahu, some forty miles from Kekaiomā-mala, there was a ferocious surf known in the old days throughout the islands for its huge and thundering waves. Today it has the same reputation among modern surfers; it is called Sunset Beach. In earlier times it was called Paumalū, which literally means "taken secretly," referring to how a woman who caught more octopus than was permitted had her legs bitten off by a shark. And according to legend, a prince of Kaua'i named Kahikilani crossed the hundred miles of open sea between his home and O'ahu just to prove his prowess in the great Paumalū surf.[6]

As soon as he arrived he started surfing. Day after day he perfected his skill in the jawlike waves. As he rode he was watched by a bird maiden with supernatural powers who lived in a cave on a nearby mountain. She fell in love with the prince and sent bird messengers to place an orange lehua lei around his neck and bring him to her. By flying around his head, the messengers guided Kahikilani to the bird maiden's cave. Enchanted, he spent several months with her—until the return of the surfing season. Then the distant sizzle and boom of the waves at Paumalū were too much for Kahikilani to resist, and he left the maiden, but only after promising never to kiss another woman. However, the excitement of the rising surf must have clouded his memory because almost as soon as he was riding again, a beautiful woman came walking along the white sand. She saw him there, waited until he rode to shore, placed an ilima lei around his neck, and kissed him. His vow was broken. He thought nothing of it and paddled back out to the breaking waves, but the bird messengers were watching. They flew to tell their mistress of his infidelity. When she heard their report, the bird maiden ran to the beach with a lehua lei in her hand. Snatching the ilima lei from Kahikilani's neck, she replaced it with the one made from lehua blossoms. As she ran back to her cave, he chased her. That was the last Kahikilani saw of the bird maiden, though, for halfway up the mountain he was turned to stone.*

---

*Kahikilani still sits today with a petrified lehua lei around his neck on a barren ridge above Paumalū Bay, less than a mile from the Kamehameha Highway. Someone has renamed his image the George Washington Stone.

Native legends abound with the exploits of those who attained distinction among their fellows by their skill and daring in this sport, indulged in alike by both sexes; and frequently too—as in these days of intellectual development—the gentler sex carried off the highest honors.[7]

This equality and sexual freedom added zest to the sport and were important to its widespread popularity. No doubt many an amorous Hawaiian, who on some day didn't feel at all like surfing, found himself paddling for the breaker line in pursuit of his lady love, knowing full well that if a man and woman happened to ride the same wave together, custom allowed certain intimacies when they returned to the beach. More formal courtship was also carried out in the surf, when a man or woman tried to woo and win a mate by performing on the waves. Hawaiian legends abound in tales of thwarted and suc-

THIS IDEALIZED WAHINE WAS SKETCHED BY JACQUES ARAGO IN HAWAI'I AROUND 1819 AND APPEARED IN HIS *RECOLLECTIONS OF A BLIND MAN*, AN ACCOUNT OF A TOUR AROUND THE WORLD. IN 1820 CHRISTIAN MISSIONARIES BEGAN ARRIVING IN THE ISLANDS, AND WITH THE ENSUING "INCREASE IN MODESTY," SCENES LIKE THIS ONE WERE SELDOM SEEN AGAIN.

cessful love affairs, and surfing played a part in many of them. Great romances could blossom or fade with the rising and falling of the ocean swells. Passionate adventures of champion surfers and famous courtships that began on the edge of the ocean were recorded in Hawai'i's abundant oral traditions. Many of these words were written down in the last century by the first generation of literate Hawaiian scholars.

For example, in *The Hawaiian Romance of Lā'ieikawai*, first published in Hawaiian by Haleole in 1863, Hauailiki, a champion surfer from the island of Kaua'i traveled to Ke'eau, Hawai'i, to court the lovely Lā'ieikawai.[8] On the fifth day of his stay, after all attempts to attract her attention had failed, he decided to try impressing her with his famous skill on a surfboard. He paddled out where he was sure she would see him. After waiting until all the other surfers had ridden away, he caught a great wave and sped gracefully to shore. Neither this spectacular ride nor the following ones earned even a glance from the beautiful maid. As a last resort, Hauailiki left his board in the sand and went body-surfing. He performed so well on several waves that Lā'ieikawai finally called him to her. As was her custom for those who surfed well, she presented him with a lehua lei. But this small token was all he ever received from her for his championship skill, and Hauailiki returned to Kaua'i empty-handed.

In another legend of courtship, the surfer in the story is a woman, Kelea, from Maui. A beautiful sister of the island's ruling chief, Kelea was famed as the most graceful and daring surf rider in the kingdom. While surfing one day at Lāhainā, she accepted the offer of a visiting O'ahu chief to ride waves in his canoe. Before they had caught many waves a sudden squall came up and blew the small craft out to sea, and Kalamakua, the visiting chief, took advantage of the storm to abduct her. As they sailed away, Kelea was told she would be the

Ka'ahumanu, expert surfer and favorite wife of Kamehameha, from *Voyage Pittoresque* by Louis Choris (1822). Photo courtesy Bishop Museum, Honolulu.

wife of Lolāle, high chief of O'ahu. At first she was infuriated, but finally she gave in to the situation and willingly became the high chief's wife. Unfortunately, Lolāle disliked the sea and preferred living inland. Thus confined far from the ocean, Kelea longed for the surf and was only happy on her occasional visits to the white beaches at 'Ewa, where she rode with Kalamakua. At last in desperation she vowed to return to her native island and leave Lolāle forever. On her return to Maui, however, she stopped at 'Ewa for one last wave, and Kalamakua proposed to her. Kelea accepted and so became the wife of the chief and fellow-surfer who had first stolen her away.[9]

AN ENGRAVING OF THE HIGH CHIEF AND GREAT SURFER KAMEHAMEHA I, ALSO FROM *VOYAGE PITTORESQUE* BY LOUIS CHORIS. PHOTO COURTESY BISHOP MUSEUM, HONOLULU.

THE ALI'I

Of all the Hawaiians who surfed, it was the *ali'i* or hereditary chiefly class who claimed the highest reputation for dedicated proficiency with board and wave. Freed from the daily chores of farming and fishing, the ali'i embraced the challenge of such sports as surfing, *hōlua*-sledding,* and canoe-leaping. They were a majestic aristocracy, often taller, broader, and stronger than the commoners. Their status as leaders depended, in part, on their strength and stamina. Strenuous sports such as surfing therefore served to keep them fit for the physical requirements of their chiefly position, as well as to furnish them with many hours of enjoyment.

Typical of the ali'i was Kaumuali'i, ruling chief of Kaua'i, whom the British missionary Ellis reported to be one of the finest surfers in all the islands. Concerning two chiefs from the island of Hawai'i, Ellis wrote:

"We have seen Karaimoku and Kakioeva, some of the highest chiefs in the island, both between fifty and sixty years of age, and large corpulent men, balancing themselves on their long and narrow boards, or splashing about in the foam, with as much satisfaction as youths of sixteen."[10]

King Kamehameha I was trained in his youth to surf with both canoe and board, and he and his favorite wife, Ka'ahumanu, were experts on waves, especially at the sport of *lele wa'a* or canoe-leaping. In lele wa'a, the surfer leaped from a canoe with his or her board into a cresting ocean swell and rode it to shore. It was a good trick when you consider that the board of an ali'i might weigh well over one hundred pounds.

Often a surf-riding chief had a personal surf chant that proclaimed his glory and skill. It had to be delivered by a chanter, and every chief kept one in his retinue. On one occasion such a chant not only glorified the chief but saved his life as well.

Naihe was a champion surfer of Ka'ū on the island of Hawai'i. According to legend, Naihe was so expert a surfer that his fellow chiefs grew jealous. They plotted to lure him into a surfing contest and then kill him. After inviting Naihe to a match at Hilo, they secretly agreed that no participant, once he had paddled out to the breakers, could return to the beach until he heard his personal chant from the shore.

---

* The art of sliding down grassy slopes or specially constructed stone ramps covered with dirt and grass, using a long, narrow wooden sled (*papa hōlua*).

The contest had already started when Naihe arrived. Although his chanter was with him, Naihe, in ignorance of the secret pact, let the old woman sleep while he paddled out. He was already in the water when he learned of the rule and was, therefore, marooned far offshore. But a chief from nearby Puna decided to aid him and sent a servant to wake Naihe's chanter. When she learned of her master's plight, she rushed to the beach. With tears streaming down her withered cheeks, the old woman stood on shore and chanted:

The great waves, the great waves rise in Kona,

Bring forth the loin cloth that it may be on display,

The ebbing tide swells to set the loin cloth flying,

The loin cloth, Hoaka, that is worn on the beach,

It is the loin cloth to wear at sea, a chief's loin cloth,

Stand up and gird on the loin cloth

The day is a rough one, befitting Naihe's surfboard,

He leaps in, he swims, he strides out to the waves,

The waves that rush hither from Kahiki.

White-capped waves, billowy waves,

Waves that break into a heap, waves that break and spread.

The surf rises above them all,

The rough surf of the island

The great surf that pounds and thrashes

The foamy surf of Hikiau,

It is the sea on which to surf at noon,

The sea that washes the pebbles and corals ashore. . . .[11]

Naihe was thus allowed to return to shore, and the plot to kill him was foiled. In the late nineteenth century, King Kalākaua, the last king of Hawai'i, adopted Naihe's surfing chant to serve as his own. Queen Emma, another member of nineteenth-century Hawaiian royalty, also had a surf chant in her honor.

Ali'i privileges in the sport went far beyond owning personal surfing chants. In one legend, for instance, a handsome surfer is almost executed for riding on the same wave at Waikīkī with a high-ranking chiefess.[12] One festive day Pīkoi, a kupua hero famed for his beauty as well as his skill at shooting rats with bow and arrow, wandered down to what is now the Moana Hotel beach. In the waves offshore a high-ranking chiefess, the wife of the island's ruling chief, was surfing with her retinue. Pīkoi, wearing a striking lei made from orange lehua blossoms, watched the chiefess catch a high blue-green wave and ride it all the way to the water's edge in front of him. As she walked ashore he asked to borrow her board, but the chiefess said the board was *kapu* (taboo) to all but herself. If he rode it, she explained, her servants would kill him. Instead she offered him the board of a chief who had just surfed to shore behind her.

Pīkoi paddled out, but there were no good waves breaking except those reserved for the chiefess, so he allowed a wave to carry him into the forbidden surf. The chiefess, pleased by his great beauty, had entered the water again and was surfing alone. As he neared her board she asked for one of his orange lehua leis. He couldn't give her one because, as he said, "You are kapu."

"Nothing is kapu for me to receive," she replied. "It will only be kapu after I have worn it." Persuaded, Pīkoi lifted a garland from his neck and gave it to her. (Later, that part of Waikīkī's surf became known as Ka-lehua-wehe, "the removed lehua.")

Then Pīkoi asked the chiefess to ride to shore on the first wave of a huge set swelling behind them. He would follow on the second. But she waited, and when Pīkoi streaked past on the second wave, she paddled and caught it behind him. Realizing the danger of riding the same wave with the chiefess, he tried to cut across from that wave to another. She skillfully caught that one, too, and, unfortunately for Pīkoi, they glided to the beach together.

A great cry rose from the revelers on shore. "That boy has broken the kapu!" The ruling chief heard the shout, looked seaward, saw the glistening bodies of his wife and Pīkoi, and called his officers. Seizing Pīkoi as he stepped from his board, they beat him and were ready to kill him when he cried, "Stop! Wait until I have spoken with the high chief!"

They stopped and dragged him into the royal presence. As he pled his case someone recognized him as the famous rat-killer. To identify himself he immediately skewered four hundred rats on a single arrow in one shot. Then a chief recognized the accused as the brother of his wife, and Pīkoi was saved.

His near execution suggests that certain breaks or boards or both were reserved for the aliʻi. Other evidence for chiefly privilege includes Ellis's observation from the 1820s that commoners avoided approaching a surfing place when the chiefs were enjoying themselves "lest they should spoil the sport" and indications that one of the two main types of surfboards were reserved for the aliʻi.

Papa heʻe nalu (wave-sliding board) was the general term for surfboards, of which there were two main types: *alaia* and *olo*. These share only one common feature: their lenticular cross-sections. In both, top and bottom were convex, tapering to thin rounded edges. Otherwise, as can be seen by glancing at the drawings of olo and alaia from Honolulu's Bishop Museum (fig. 5), they were radically different in form—and, as we shall explain, in function as well.

The alaia boards are round-nosed with a squared-off tail and very thin. The larger alaia boards in the Bishop's collection range from seven to twelve feet long, average eighteen inches in width, and are from a half inch to an inch and a half thick. (The museum's shorter alaia-shaped boards, which can be classified as bodyboards because of their lack of buoyancy, are similarly proportioned.) Most alaia boards that have survived are made from koa (*Acacia koa*), a fine-grained Hawaiian hardwood, although various writers state that alaia were also made from such light woods as breadfruit (*Artocarpus altila*) and wiliwili (*Erythrina sandwicensis*).

The olo is a very long, thick and heavy board, yet proportionately narrow. Although one nineteenth-century writer claimed that olo boards could be as long as four fathoms (twenty-four feet), the longest of the three olo in the Bishop Museum measures just over seventeen feet and is about sixteen and a half inches wide, five and three-quarters inches thick, and weighs more than 150 pounds. The board came from the collection of Prince Kūhiō, Hawaiʻi's delegate to the U.S. Congress immediately following annexation. It is made from imported pine. The other two olo boards in the Bishop Museum, one of which is featured in figure 5 as a type specimen of the olo, were owned by high chief Abner Pākī, a noted surfer who regularly rode at Waikīkī during the 1830s. Although both of Pākī's boards are made from koa, a number of nineteenth-century writers state that wiliwili wood was preferred for making olo boards because of its extreme lightness, which also makes it ideal for outrigger canoe floats. However, the

ANCIENT HAWAIIAN SURFBOARDS AND BODYBOARDS IN THE BISHOP MUSEUM COLLECTION

Figure 5.

Ancient Hawaiian Surfboards.

THESE FIVE BOARDS ARE TYPICAL OF THOSE USED BY EARLY SURFERS. THESE DIAGRAMS ARE TAKEN FROM BOARDS NOW PRESERVED IN THE BISHOP MUSEUM IN HONOLULU. THE SMALLEST WERE BODYBOARDS, PROBABLY USED BY CHILDREN. THE LARGEST, THE OLO, WERE SOMETIMES SIXTEEN FEET LONG OR MORE AND WERE USED EXCLUSIVELY BY CHIEFS. THE MOST POPULAR BOARD WAS THE SHORTER, THINNER ALAIA.

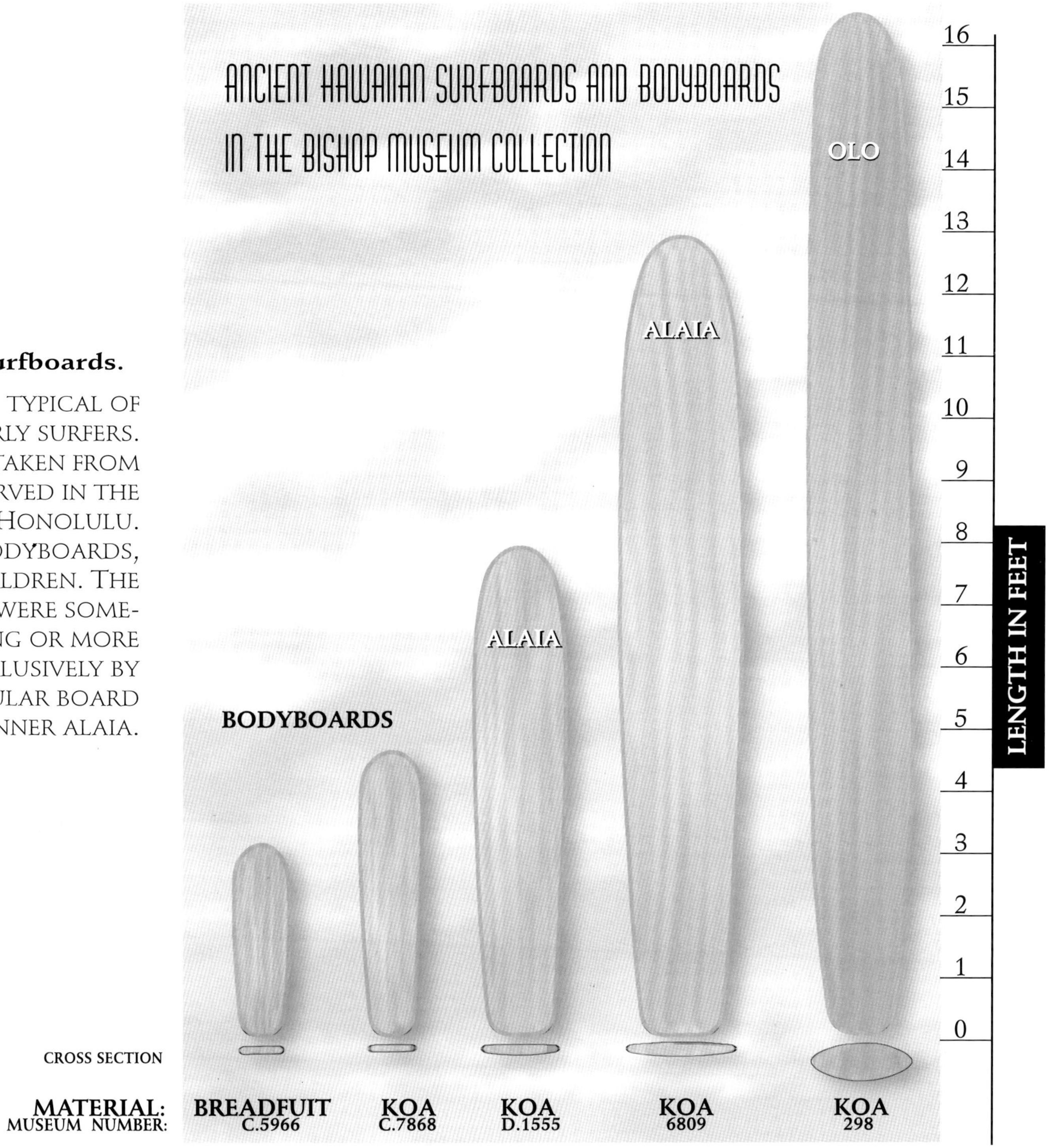

OLO

ALAIA

ALAIA

BODYBOARDS

LENGTH IN FEET

16
15
14
13
12
11
10
9
8
7
6
5
4
3
2
1
0

CROSS SECTION

MATERIAL:	BREADFUIT	KOA	KOA	KOA	KOA
MUSEUM NUMBER:	C.5966	C.7868	D.1555	6809	298

light, porous wiliwili is more perishable than koa, which probably explains why there are no wiliwili boards in the museum's collection.*

Because of its great length and buoyancy the olo was especially adapted for riding large, humping swells such as those that occur at Waikīkī. We have no eyewitness descriptions of olo surfing, but experiments conducted at Waikīkī during the 1930s with sixteen-foot hollow boards give us

ABNER PĀKĪ (C. 1808–1855) WAS A HIGH CHIEF IN THE FIRST HALF OF THE NINETEENTH CENTURY AND A NOTED SURFER AT WAIKĪKĪ DURING THE 1830S. PHOTO COURTESY BISHOP MUSEUM, HONOLULU.

some insight into the advantages and disadvantages of such massive long boards. Their buoyancy allowed the rider to catch a swell long before it broke and much farther out to sea than was possible with shorter boards. Once on a wave, a surfer could slide with ease until long after the wave had crested and begun to flatten out. An olo might even catch a wave that began to peak but never broke, as often happens at Waikīkī when the swell is weak. Once on a wave, however, with the ride's angle set, the surfer could not make fast turns, especially when the wave grew steep. Also, a huge board was hard to paddle through breaking waves to the *kūlana nalu*, the take-off point, requiring a surfer to paddle clear around the surf line or, in the old days, to hitch a ride on a canoe to get in position beyond the breaking surf.

In contrast, the shorter and more maneuverable alaia board was ideally suited to the steeper, faster-breaking surf. Waikīkī's combination of long low swells and sandy shore is not common around the islands. Along the Kona coast of the island of Hawai'i, for example, one finds more often the rocky terrain described by Lieutenant King, with steep walls of water breaking closer to shore. The alaia's shorter length and thinness gave it the mobility needed to negotiate the sheer faces of such fast-breaking waves. Crucial was the technique called *lala* of sliding at an angle along the face of the moving swell. An eyewitness report of an Hawaiian on a seven-foot alaia board at Hilo, Hawai'i, in 1878 said:

One instantly dashed in, in front of and at the lowest declivity of the advancing wave, and with a few strokes of the hands and feet established his position; then without further effort shot along the base of the wave eastward with incredible velocity. . . . his course was along the foot of the wave, and parallel to it. . . . so as soon as the bather had secured his position he gave a spring and stood on his knees upon the board, and just as he was passing us . . . he gave another spring and stood upon his feet, now folding his arms on his breast, and now swinging them about in wild ecstasy in his exhilarating ride.[13]

Such rapid alaia-adapted surf is by far the most common that breaks in Hawai'i, even today. The surfer, of course, needed an alert dexterity to ride successfully and avoid losing his or her board or smashing it on the rocks. But the alaia's shape made it possible for the rider to avoid the tumbling crests as well as the danger of "nosing in."

*It is fitting that Pākī's boards came to be preserved in the Bishop Museum, for this repository of Polynesian culture was founded as a memorial to his daughter, Mrs. Bernice Pauahi Bishop, a descendant of King Kamehameha.

Author Ben Finney with part of the world's largest collection of ancient Hawaiian surfboards, in the Bishop Museum, Honolulu.

It was the board most suitable along the frequent rugged coasts, and it is no wonder that most of the ancient boards remaining (ten of thirteen in the Bishop Museum collection) are of the alaia type. All the early reports of this sport seem to focus on surfing alaia style, and many legends mention chiefs surfing along rocky shores where an olo board would be difficult to handle.

However, whereas both the chiefly class and commoners surfed on alaia boards, the right to ride the majestic olo boards may have been reserved exclusively for the ali'i. In a late-nineteenth-century account of surfing (see Appendix E), its Hawaiian author states unequivocally that "it is well know that the olo was only for the use of chiefs; none of the common people use it."[14] Although no other writers were so explicit on this point, excluding commoners from riding olo boards makes sense when we consider the structure of Hawaiian society along with the unique riding characteristics of these boards. In ancient Hawai'i the ali'i formed an exclusive class with special rights and privileges with respect to the commoners, the *maka'āinana*. So unequal were the two classes that a commoner might be put to death for transgressing, even accidentally, on the person or property of a high-ranking chief.[15] In such a highly stratified society it would be hard to imagine how a commoner, surfing at Waikīkī for example, could ride an olo board, particularly when chiefs were also surfing there. A commoner who had caught a large swell far outside and had taken his angle might have found himself bearing down on a chiefly surfer straining to catch the same swell with an alaia board or paddling out through the surf. Since the commoner would not have been able to turn an olo board fast enough, any chiefly surfer in his way would have been forced either to paddle furiously to avoid a collision or, if too late for that, to dive overboard to avoid injury—an unthinkable situation in ancient Hawaiian society.

Because of the difficulty of handling these huge boards, modern surfers have generally considered the olo a curiosity—interesting, but poorly adapted for fast-breaking waves. In the 1960s, however, surfers seeking a way to ride the untested fifty-foot monsters that crash into Ka'ena Point on O'ahu began to reconsider the olo's merits. Perhaps, they thought, in its extreme length and narrowness lies the secret. With their own big-wave boards, which measured eleven feet or so, they knew that even if they could catch a Ka'ena Point monster, they would only be able to do so just before it crested—and that they would die in the next moment when tons of water slammed over them. But they theorized that a long, buoyant olo might enable them to catch such a giant wave when the swell was still comparatively flat, then stand, take an angle, and ride across and out before it could reach its critical steepness.

No one has yet had the courage to test this. If ever proven it will certainly open the possibility that ancient Hawaiians surfed waves as big or perhaps bigger than those now attempted by surfers on O'ahu's north shore.

COMPETITION

Whichever board they chose, the chiefs took great pride in the skill, grace, speed, and courage with which they rode the Pacific's swells. They frequently performed in public, and such displays were not always to court a visiting chiefess from another island. Hawaiian surfers often exhibited their finest wave-riding style in fierce competition. This was, in fact, a major part of the game to early enthusiasts, and the betting that accompanied every contest was no doubt an important incentive for the practice of the sport.

Before a surfing contest in which chiefs were competing, a dog might be buried in an underground oven and baked, so that the contestants could periodically replenish their strength during the match. If the contest was one of pride, the chiefs would gird themselves in tapa loincloths dyed red. When preliminaries were over and all the bets were in, the competing surfers paddled out to a predetermined position to wait for a swell to come through. As soon as a large wave rose up behind them they paddled, caught it together, and rode until they reached a *pua* (buoy) anchored inshore. The first man to the pua won the heat. Probably several such rides determined the winner of the contest.

In addition to this surfer-versus-surfer competition, there was another kind of match, which pitted a chief's surfboard against a land-locked hōlua sled. At Keauhou on Hawai'i, in the 1960s one could still see a stone hōlua slide stretching several hundred yards down a mountain slope to the shore at He'eia Bay. A grass house once squatted at the bottom of the slide, and beyond the house, out to sea, a famous surf broke. During the competition, when a large wave approached the breaking place, someone would flash a white tapa flag from the grass house. Then a young chief at the top of the slide would run a few powerful steps, throw himself and his narrow sled belly-down on the slide, and plummet seaward. At the same time, out at sea, a surfer would catch the wave that had triggered the signal and race the sled to shore. The first to reach the grass hut was the winner.

Wagering on such matches, by contestants as well as spectators, was a favorite and often fanatic pastime that occasionally overshadowed the sport itself. "Surf-riding was a national sport of the Hawaiians," wrote the nineteenth-century Hawaiian scholar David Malo, "on which they were very fond of betting, each man staking his property on the one thought to be most skillful."[16] And, "Hawaiians were much addicted to gambling, even to the last article they possessed." This passion is unusual in comparison to Polynesia's other island groups, where betting was unknown or much less important. Overcome by the excitement of an ensuing contest, a Hawaiian might impetuously wager canoes, fishing nets and lines, tapa cloth, swine, and sometimes his own life or personal freedom, all on the outcome of the match.

The dangers of such a contest are illustrated in the legendary match that once took place between Umi-a-līloa, a great chief of Hawai'i, and Paiea, a lesser chief. Before he became high chief, Umi attended a surfing match at Laupāhoehoe, Hawai'i. While there he was challenged to a contest by Paiea. Because of the small wager Paiea proposed, Umi refused the offer. When Paiea upped his bet to four double-hulled canoes, Umi accepted. He then defeated Paiea and won the four canoes, but during the match Paiea's surfboard had clipped Umi on the shoulder, scratching off some skin. Umi said nothing at the time, but when he later came to power as high chief he had Paiea killed and sacrificed to his god at the *heiau* (temple) at Waipunalei.[17]

CONSECRATION, CONSTRUCTION, AND THE GODS

Surfing was, on one hand, a popular recreation. But when a scratch on the shoulder might lead to death, or, as in Naihe's case, when one's skill could excite jealous chiefs to an assassination plot, it could also be a rather serious affair. This was especially true as it entwined itself with other vital elements of Hawaiian culture. In this sense, it was connected with the ancient religion of the islands. Although surfing was not specifically a religious observance, it was, like other aspects of Hawaiian life, integrally involved with the gods and spirits of the day.

The observance of ritual began when a potential surfboard was still an image in the craftsman's mind; it began with the tree. When he had selected a suitable koa or wiliwili tree, a board builder placed a red fish at its trunk. He then cut down the tree with a stone ax, dug a hole among the roots, and placed the fish therein with a prayer as an offering to the gods in return for the tree he was about to shape into a board. The construction and shaping of the surfboard that followed this ritual was an exacting task that required the experienced craftsmanship of professional board builders.

The trunk was first chipped away with an ax and roughly shaped to the desired dimensions. It was then pulled down to the beach and placed in a hālau (canoe house) for finishing work. To remove the uneven surface of ax marks, the board was smoothed with rough coral. Stone rubbers called 'ōahi were used to polish the boards, much as canoe hulls were polished. As a finishing stain, the root of the ti plant or the juice of pounded kukui bark was used to give the completed board a dark, glistening luster. Stains were also obtained from the soot of burned kukui nuts, charcoal from burnt pandanus leaves, or the juices from young banana buds. To complete the process, a dressing of kukui nut oil was applied when the stain was dry, and the black, glossy board was ready. Before it was set in the water there were still other rites and ceremonies to be performed in dedicating the board to insure its wave-riding success. And although the common people often disregarded these observances, professional board builders followed them faithfully.

Once completed, a board is of little use to the surfer unless the surf is running. When the ocean was flat the Hawaiians took measures to secure the return of ridable waves. If a group of surfers wanted to address the ocean, they might gather on the beach, find strands of pōhuehue (beach morning glory), swing them around their heads together, and lash the surface of the water chanting in unison. One such surf chant has been recorded and translated as follows:

Kū mai! Kū mai! Ka nalu nui mai Kahiki mai,

Alo po'i pu! Kū mai ka pō huehue,

Hū ! Kaiko'o loa.

Arise! Arise, ye great surfs from Kahiki,

The powerful curling waves.

Arise with pōhuehue

Well up, long raging surf.[18]

Surfing also played a part in the annual celebration the Hawaiians called *Makahiki*. The great god Lono was the patron deity of those festivities. From mid October to early February, the Hawaiians stopped work, relaxed, and passed much of their time dancing, feasting, and participating in sports. Thousands gathered to watch the famous tournaments, which always included surfing, and a special god of sport (*akua pa'ani*) presided over each contest. Of such festivals and Hawaiian sports and games in general, Kenneth Emory wrote:

> No important contest was engaged in without approaching the gods with prayers and offerings to win their favor. Some god presided over every sport. When a man felt he was in harmonious relations with the mysterious forces about him he was quite likely to accomplish superhuman feats of strength and skill.[19]

Among the many Hawaiian gods and their multitudinous aspects, however, there is no specific mention of a special god for surfing. In Tahiti, Ellis tells us, the presiding god of surfing was Huaouri. Unfortunately, his Hawaiian counterpart, who can only be inferred, remains nameless and unknown. But this possibility of a surfing god is strengthened by the existence on the island of Hawai'i of at least one stone temple that was dedicated to surfing.

A heiau was an ancient Hawaiian shrine or place of worship. It might be built in connection with a community, an individual deity, or a certain activity. At Kahalu'u Bay on the Kona coast stands a large structure built of lichen-spotted black lava rock, which was well known to local Hawaiians questioned in the early 1900s as a surfing heaiu where one might pray for good surf.[20] The stone pool nearby was said to be convenient for rinsing salt water from one's body after surfing. This structure, called Ku'emanu Heiau, still exists today, fairly well preserved. It consists mainly of an upper stone terrace which rests on a larger foundation. A deep, stone-lined water pool, ideal for bathing, is sunk into one side of the foundation terrace. A surf, which legends suggest was well known to ancient Hawaiians, still breaks offshore at Ku'emanu, directly in front of the heiau. The stone terraces are so aligned that from the upper level, spectators might easily watch surfers riding waves less than a hundred yards away.

This site is remarkably similar to Keolonāhihi Heiau, which fronts the sea at Hōlualoa, a few miles north of Kahalu'u. It also features a pool and bleacherlike terraces and faces a once well-known surfing area. King Kamehameha learned to surf at Keolonāhihi, and local chiefs favored the surrounding lands for their abundant food resources and the presence of good surfing waves.

These old heiau are overgrown and obscured in places by tropical vegetation. Even so, sitting now on those stony terraces, gazing into the still reflection of the bathing pool or watching a well-formed wave crumble just offshore, one cannot help but speculate upon the rites that may have preceded a famous contest or followed a long run of exhilarating surf. It is easy enough to imagine the rows of polished koa boards and the chanters who accompanied the supple ali'i who must have gathered there.*

In religion, in language, in festivals, in love, and in song and story, surfing was woven into the life of ancient Hawai'i. Its related activities overlapped one another in the complexities and contradictions of the old social order: a surfer might sweat for weeks shaping and shining a new board to perfection, then avoid work of any kind for days on end as he joined his fellow villagers in the mounting surf. He might dedicate his alaia to the gods and then gamble his life away in the riding of it. With chants, contests, ten dozen places to surf, and literally thousands of hand-carved boards to ride upon, surfing was truly the sport of commoners as well as chiefs—a vital part of the isolated island world European voyagers chanced upon in 1778.

---

* In the late 1970s Ku'emanu Heiau was rescued from developers and turned into a protected monument.

AN ENGRAVING OF THE VISITING BRITISH MISSIONARY WILLIAM ELLIS PREACHING IN KAILUA ON THE ISLAND OF HAWAI'I.
PHOTO COURTESY BISHOP MUSEUM, HONOLULU.

CHAPTER FOUR

The Touch Of Civilization

The palaces of kings are built upon the ruins of the bowers of paradise.

—THOMAS PAINE

From the peak in its development, surfing suddenly and very rapidly began to decline. During the nineteenth century the sport almost completely disappeared, and by 1900 a wave, a board, and a surfer were seldom seen together on the foamy edges of Hawai'i's green islands. As early as 1844, in a volume called *Scenes and Scenery in the Sandwich Islands*, one observer noted that surfing was already a rare sight. Ten years later, another observer noted that Lāhainā, Maui, was one of the few places left in the islands where waves were still ridden with any enthusiasm. At Hilo, perhaps one of the last strongholds of surfing on the island of Hawai'i, another writer observed in 1876 that although one could still watch the grand spectacle there, few of the younger generation had learned how to surf and those who had were undistinguished.[1]

As the century wore on, the scenes that William Ellis had witnessed in the 1820s—of whole villages dropping everything to surf and of corpulent, aging chiefs riding the waves with the joy of youths—became just fading memories. More and more waves were rolling in unridden to bury themselves on Hawai'i's beaches. What happened to the thousands and thousands of gleaming surfboards? What caused the Hawaiians to abandon the sport that they alone had developed to such a peak through so many generations? To understand the reasons, we must consider surfing within the framework of Hawaiian culture and society and the damage wrought by the coming of Europeans with their diseases, weapons, consumer goods, institutions, and ideologies.

Surfing's decline was part of the wider disaster visited upon the Hawaiian people. From the arrival of the first Europeans in 1778 to the American takeover of the islands in 1898, virtually all native sports and pastimes declined to the point of disappearance as Hawaiians lost their social, economic, and political independence and their numbers were steadily reduced by disease. This tragedy began with the arrival of the British ships commanded by Capt. James Cook. The isolated Hawaiians, lacking any natural immunity to the infectious diseases carried by the British and the succession of seamen, whalers, and adventurers from many nations who followed, were struck down in great numbers by measles, small pox, and other diseases previously unknown in Hawai'i. Imported venereal diseases then sterilized many of the survivors. By the 1890s, this biological onslaught had reduced the Hawaiian population from the 400,000 estimated by Lieutenant King in 1779 to around 40,000, a drop of 90 percent.* Furthermore, by "discovering" Hawai'i and mapping its location for the Western world, the British opened the islands to a parade of *Haole*—Europeans, Americans, and other foreigners of European extraction—whose activities transformed life in the islands. Sandalwood traders,

---

* Estimates of the pre-European population of Hawai'i range from as low as 200,000 to as high as 800,000; whatever the figure, the reduction to 40,000 was catastrophic.

BY THE END OF THE NINETEENTH CENTURY, WHEN THIS PHOTO WAS TAKEN, SURFING WAS AT ITS LOWEST EBB. THIS LONE HAWAIIAN SURFER AT WAIKĪKĪ BEACH CARRIES ONE OF THE LAST ALAIA BOARDS TO BE RIDDEN THERE.

whalers, and the merchants who took up residence introduced consumer goods and the money economy. Later, American missionaries-turned-businessmen and other capitalists bought up Hawaiian lands to develop a sugar industry; in so doing they imported so many laborers from Asia that by the 1890s the Hawaiians had become a minority in their own land. While this transformation was unfolding, the earnest attempt by Hawaiians to take their place among the community of nations—as an independent kingdom ruled by the Kamehameha dynasty—was being undermined by Haole sugar planters and businessmen who had become Hawaiian citizens and had gained elective or appointive office. When Queen Lili'uokalani attempted to roll back Haole control of the kingdom in 1893, the foreigners staged a revolution. Aided by the intimidating presence of a force of U.S. Marines landed from an American naval vessel, they overthrew the monarchy, established a republic, and in 1898 succeeded in having Hawai'i annexed by the United States.

In this process of radical change, Hawaiian culture and values came under heavy attack, first indirectly and then directly. The arrival of foreigners with their ships, guns, and seemingly wondrous goods led Hawaiians to doubt the power of their gods and ultimately themselves. That these foreigners could be so powerful and wealthy without respecting the kapu system, the sacred taboos that had regulated every aspect of island life, led daring Hawaiians to flout specific prohibitions until finally, the king uprooted the entire system. One day in 1819, Liholiho, Kamehameha I's son and successor, sat down to eat with his mother and other high-ranking chiefesses, deliberately breaking the all-important kapu against men and women eating together. This was a public sign that the kapu system was to be abandoned and that people were no longer under the power of the old gods.

Overthrowing the kapu system cut the Hawaiians adrift from the power of their gods and the stability of ritual regulation, disorganizing family and class structure and impacting farming, fishing, and all other aspects of daily life. As far as sport and games were concerned, the most immediate effect of the 1819 revolution was the lapse of the annual Makahiki festival intimately tied to the god Lono. Celebrated fully for the last time just before his overthrow, the Makahiki's lusty stimulus had been of prime importance in keeping sports and games alive and fresh and in maintaining public support. With the end of the festival the great tournaments were never organized again, and Hawaiian sports were never again inspired by the mass enthusiasm of the Makahiki. For surfing, the abolition of the traditional religion signaled the end of its sacred aspects. With surf chants, board construction rites, sports gods, and other sacred elements removed, the once ornate sport of surfing was stripped of much of its cultural plumage.

To complete this denuding, a new religion arrived with a new god and a whole new system of restrictions to replace Hawai'i's decaying worship forms. In 1820, the year following the overthrow of the kapu system, American missionaries from New England landed and set out to convert the Hawaiians. Though initially unsuccessful, within the decade the missionaries had converted key chiefs and chiefesses, and during the 1830s they succeeded in establishing their Calvinistic brand of Christianity as the new religion of the islands.

Basic to their teachings was an abhorrence of pastimes that took people away from work and worship. As early as 1838, a visitor who called on Hawai'i during a round-the-world cruise, noted that:

A change has taken place in certain customs. . . . I allude to the variety of athletic exercises, such as swimming, with or without a surfboard, dancing, wrestling, throwing the javelin, etc., all of which games, being in opposition to the strict te-

A MISSIONARY PREACHES TO
A HAWAIIAN CONGREGATION 1820s.
PHOTO COURTESY BISHOP MUSEUM, HONOLULU.

nets of Calvinism, have been suppressed. . . . Can the missionaries be fairly charged with suppressing these games? I believe they deny having done so. But they write and publicly express their opinions, and state these sports to be expressly against the laws of God, and by a succession of reasoning, which may readily be traced, impress upon the minds of the chiefs and others, the idea that all who practice them, secure themselves the displeasure of offended heaven. Then the chiefs, for a spontaneous benevolence, at once interrupt customs so hazardous to their vassals."[2]

Defending missionary policy in those early days was Hiram Bingham, who protested that the churchmen were innocent of suppressing Hawaiian pastimes. Concerning surfing he wrote:

The decline and discontinuance of the use of the surfboard, as civilization advances, may be accounted for by the increase in modesty, industry and religion, without supposing, as some have affected to believe, that missionaries caused oppressive enactments against it.[3]

By the modesty of a new life he meant the adoption of European clothing, which was not nearly so convenient as a loincloth for swimming and surfing. To illustrate their increase in industry he singled out the time-consuming process of making a new cloth garment or earning money to buy one, and the chief's demands

on commoners' labor for purchasing European merchandise. His reference to religion apparently meant that the requirements of the new faith left little time for leisure.

Another aspect of the missionaries' righteous attitude was voiced by Sheldon Dibble when, speaking of "rough" sports such as surfing, he wrote:

The evils resulting from all these sports and amusement have in part been named. Some lost their lives thereby, some were severely wounded, maimed and crippled; some were reduced to poverty, both by losses in gambling and by neglecting to cultivate the land; and the instances were not few in which they were reduced to utter starvation. But the greatest evil of all resulted from the constant intermingling, without any restraint, of persons of both sexes and of all ages, at all times of the day and at all hours of the night.[4]

Of course, surfing itself did not displease all the missionaries, but they were unanimously united in their opposition to the re-

HIRAM BINGHAM, CHIEF AMERICAN MISSIONARY, PREACHING AT WAIMEA DURING A TOUR OF O'AHU IN 1826. SEATED NEXT TO HIM IS KA'AHUMANU, THE WIDOW OF KAMEHAMEHA I AND AN EARLY CHRISTIAN CONVERT. PHOTO COURTESY BISHOP MUSEUM, HONOLULU.

FULLY DRESSED IN EUROPEAN FINERY, MEMBERS OF HAWAIIAN ROYALTY LEAVE CHURCH AFTER SERVICES, MID 1830S. PHOTO COURTESY BISHOP MUSEUM, HONOLULU.

lated activities such as betting, the "immorality" of surfing together in "scanty costume," sexual freedom among men and women surfers, and whatever religious practices might have remained after the collapse of the old religion.

With these activities forbidden, interest in surfing quickly died. The Hawaiians apparently found little value in the sport when it lacked these attractions. One explanation of the decline admits that, "as the zest of the sport was enhanced by the fact that both sexes engaged in it, when this practice was found to be discountenanced by the new morality, it was felt that the interest in it had largely departed—and this game too went the way of its fellows."[5] The same reaction greeted the prohibition of gambling. The life seemed to go out of surfing and those other sports in which competition and betting had been important. Afterward their practice was dull and unexciting.

In addition to the loss of these flavoring elements, foreigners introduced new recreational activities that interested the Western-conscious Hawaiians and in many cases served as substitutes for their traditional games. For instance, playing cards probably influenced the early disappearance of *kōnane*, a game similar to checkers, and *pūhenehene*, a guessing game in which objects are concealed on a player's body. The introduction of the horse brought about the end of *heihei kūkini*, or foot racing; thereafter horse riding and racing competed with swimming and surfing for Hawaiians' leisure time and energy.

While learning new games the Hawaiians also were preoccupied with understanding and adapting to a new life; this further contributed to the neglect and disappearance of old pastimes. The new learning brought by missionaries was an imposing challenge to the islanders. Curious about the previously unimagined secrets of reading and writing, and encouraged or ordered by their chiefs, many Hawaiians undertook the arduous task of learning the scholarly skills of the West

and quickly achieved a literacy rate that surpassed that of the United States. Evidently they rated the new learning above their traditional pleasures, at least sometimes: in one hastily constructed nineteenth-century schoolhouse on Kaua'i, surfboards were used to build writing tables and seats!

Given the onslaught of infectious diseases; the loss of land, livelihood, and sovereignty; the abandonment of an encouraging traditional religion followed by the embrace of a dour alien creed; and then the enticement of new activities; it is a wonder that all traditional Hawaiian sports and pastimes did not disappear. Surfing actually fared better than most, although by the turn of the century it was on its way to extinction, according to some observers.

To see what might have happened in Hawai'i, let us leap for a moment two thousand miles south to Tahiti, where another Polynesian community suffered a similar encounter with the outside world. As we have seen, of all the places where surfing was enjoyed in the Pacific, Tahiti ranked second only to Hawai'i in the sport's development. Men and women as well as children enjoyed it, and the more expert riders could stand on their boards. When one of the authors visited Tahiti with his surfboard in the mid 1950s, all that remained of Tahitian surfing was an occasional youngster skimming through small waves on a bodyboard. Not one true surfboard was to be seen on the waves that break around this fabled south sea island. The changes wrought by Western intrusion had virtually eliminated this once popular recreation. Attempts to interest Tahitians by demonstrating how to ride the beach breaks and the curling waves at the reef passes were unsuccessful. They were not interested anymore. It was a children's pastime, they said, not worth the time and effort to learn.

As long ago as 1891 surfing in Tahiti had apparently already disappeared. In that year the American historian Henry Adams observed:

As for the Tahitians that have come within my acquaintance . . . they have been the most commonplace, dreary, spiritless people I have yet seen. If they have amusements or pleasures, they conceal them. Neither dance nor game have I seen or heard of; nor surfing, swimming, nor ball-playing nor anything but the stupid, mechanical himene [hymn singing].[6]

In those days Hawaiian surfing was little better off. Just a year later, in 1892, Nathaniel Emerson wrote this of Hawai‘i:

The sport of surf-riding possessed a grand fascination, and for a time it seemed as if it had the vitality of its own as a national pastime. There are those living . . . who remember the time when almost the entire population of a village would at certain hours resort to the sea-side to indulge in, or to witness, this magnificent accomplishment. We cannot but mourn its decline. But this too has felt the touch of civilization, and today it is hard to find a surfboard outside of our museums and private collections.[7]

The museum would indeed have been an incongruous end for what was once such a vigorous and spectacular sport. Fortunately, although surfing wasted away during the nineteenth century, it did not die. He‘e nalu, in fact, fared best of all the traditional Hawaiian sports and games. Most of the others quickly disappeared early in the period of foreign contact. Surfing's flame died down, but a combination of circumstances preserved in Hawai‘i the Polynesian pastime that disappeared in such other early cultural centers as Tahiti and Aotearoa. From somewhere, a spark remained to smolder through the dark century of Hawai‘i's transformation. Nearly one hundred years after the abandonment of the kapu system—when what little that remained of the old world was almost unrecognizable—new, fresh elements in a changed Hawai‘i fanned the spark and brought surfing back to life.

Waikīkī, 1905. Photo courtesy the Baker Collection, Bishop Museum, Honolulu.

CHAPTER FIVE

The Revival

Take surf-boarding, for instance. A California real estate agent, with that one asset could make the burnt barren desert of the Sahara into an oasis for kings. Not only did the Hawaii-born not talk about it, but they forgot about it. Just as the sport was at its dying gasp, along comes one Alexander Ford from the mainland. And he talked. Surf-boarding was the sport of sports. There was nothing like it anywhere else in the world. . . . It was one of the island's assets, a drawing card that would fill the hotels and bring them many permanent residents.

—JACK LONDON, 1916

As the twentieth century began, most of the surfers left in the islands were riding at Kalehuawehe and the other surfing breaks at Waikīkī. Only a few surfers were actively riding the waves off Maui, Kaua'i and tiny Ni'ihau (the small, privately owned island near Kaua'i reserved exclusively for Hawaiians). Surfing on the once popular Kona coast of the Big Island had virtually disappeared. Although Waikīkī was certainly prominent in ancient times, the proximity of this famous beach and its many surfing breaks to the growing urban center of Honolulu probably explains why this region became the center for the sport at the turn of century. Not only had Honolulu become Hawai'i's largest city, but one out of four Hawaiians was living there. Yet even at Waikīkī there was barely a suggestion of the sport's former glory.

The large olo boards were no longer made. Although a few alaia boards might still have been in use, judging from old photographs the surfboards being made and ridden in the first years of this century were like the alaia in general outline but not in detail. They were short, around six or seven feet long and several inches thick, lacking

the finely shaped double-convex cross-section of their predecessors. In fact, many look to have been hardly more than rough-hewn planks. The surfers themselves were few in number; at Waikīkī only a handful could be seen in the water at any one time. And riding techniques seemed to have regressed. Many of these surfers rode straight-off instead of angling across the wave. No longer were there the "difficult and dangerous maneuvers" that Lieutenant King had found altogether astonishing and so hard to believe. No longer were amazed Europeans describing surfers who "shot along the base of the wave eastward with incredible velocity." The sport might be said to have returned to its infancy: boards were short, riding techniques were simple, the whole pastime was unelaborate and practiced only by a few. Soon after the turn of the century, however, the first signs of a revival appeared.

During the nineteenth century few Haole learned to handle a surfboard. Mark Twain, during his trip to Hawai'i in the 1860s, said, "None but the natives ever master the art of surf-bathing thoroughly."[1] It was a popular myth, in fact, that only a Hawaiian could balance successfully while standing and riding a wave. Despite this belief, in the early 1900s a number Honolulu residents, including many enthusiastic schoolboys,* rediscovered the waves at Waikīkī, and gradually interest in the sport was renewed. Considered as one of the best of the new surfers was George Freeth, a young Irish-Hawaiian who in 1907 left for southern California where he popularized the Hawaiian sport. Also prominent in the new movement was Alexander Hume Ford, an adventurous mainlander who was so enamored with the sport that he took it upon himself to personally boost its revival and popularization. Ford conducted surfing classes for youngsters at Waikīkī, and in 1907 he taught Jack London how to ride a surfboard. During his famous cruise on *The Snark*, London spent several weeks in Hawai'i and camped for a while in a tent on the beach at Waikīkī. One hot June afternoon he paddled out with Ford and George Freeth to watch and learn.

On that same day London's wife, Charmian, watched the surfing activity from the beach. Her descriptions of riding styles help us picture the state of wave-riding in the early days of its revival:

The thick board, somewhat coffin-shaped, with rounded ends,

SURF-BATHING—FAILURE. THIS AND "SURF-BATHING—SUCCESS" (NEXT PAGE) APPEARED IN MARK TWAIN'S BOOK *ROUGHING IT* (1872).

should be over six feet long. This plank is floated out to the breaking water, which can be done either wading alongside or lying face-downward paddling; and there you wait for the right wave. When you see it coming, stand ready to launch the board on the gathering slope, spring upon it, and—keep going if you can. Lie flat on your chest, hands grasping the sides of the large end of the heavy timber, and steer with your feet. The expert, having gauged the right speed, rises cautiously to his knees, to full stature, and then, erect with feet in the churning foam, he makes straight for the beach.[2]

It sounds tame by modern standards. Still, it was a start. Ironically enough, just as this revival was getting underway, the construction of large hotels and private residences began to close off the beachfront. The new and eager surfers, who stored their boards and changed their clothes along the unoccupied shore, were suddenly being squeezed off the beach. This might have dampened some of the burgeoning enthusiasm had not a group of newcomers from the main-

---

* One of these schoolboy surfers was Kenneth Emory, whose youthful enthusiasm for all things Hawaiian led him to become an internationally renowned scholar of Polynesian cultures. In the late 1950s he served as a supervisor of Ben Finney's dissertation on Hawaiian surfing (Finney 1959a).

land recognized the surfers' predicament and the possible danger to the sport itself, which was a tourist attraction as well as an invigorating pastime. Under the leadership of Alexander Hume Ford, this group promoted surfing's potential in a new Hawai'i. About this time, Jack London wrote an impassioned article on "A Royal Sport" that appeared in a national American magazine and spurred interest among Hawai'i's residents, as well as on the mainland (see Appendix F). Finally the surfing promoters in Honolulu acquired for lease from the Queen Emma Estate an acre of beachfront property, and on May 1, 1908, they founded the Hawaiian Outrigger Canoe Club for the purpose of "preserving surfing on boards and in Hawaiian outrigger canoes."[3] It was an unprecedented move. The club became the world's first organization whose stated mission was the perpetuation of wave-riding. It soon offered facilities for dressing and a grass hut for board storage right on the beach. This gave surfers easy access to the sand and to the long, sloping rollers.

Interest increased so rapidly that within a few months a surfing carnival was staged in honor of a visiting American battleship. And by Christmas of the same year a contest was held at Waikīkī. It was won by a fourteen-year-old Haole youth who rode the wave of the day for one hundred yards while standing on his head.

SURF-BATHING—SUCCESS

By the following summer the sport had attracted a number of Honolulu business men, as well as an ex-governor of the Islands and even some judges from the Territorial Supreme Court. That same summer, 1909, the sport enjoyed another big publicity boost when Ford himself described Hawaiian surfing in *Colliers National Weekly*,[4] which at the time was one of America's leading periodicals.

The Outrigger Club existed mainly for the Haole population of Honolulu. Three years after its foundation, a second surfing club was formed. The Hui Nalu (Surf Club) began informally around 1905 and was officially organized in 1911 to promote the sport among Hawaiians. In this way the Hawaiians eventually regained their place on the beach, and with their renewed participation and the friendly rivalry between the two clubs, the sport began to recover its status as an important part of Hawai'i's culture. In 1911 as many as one hundred surfboards could be seen at Waikīkī on a weekend.

As surfing expanded, riding skills developed. Boards grew longer. Soon boards of ten feet and more appeared at Waikīkī. A new generation of surfers rediscovered the ancient technique of *lala* and were sliding angles across the glittering slopes. In 1915 Jack London returned to Hawai'i and was amazed to find that the Outrigger Club had twelve hundred members, "with hundreds more on the waiting list, and with

what seems like half a mile of surf-board lockers."[5] During that same trip Charmian London once again described the sport, and her second account suggests what Waikīkī surfers had accomplished since her first visit:

> The newest brood of surf-boarders had learned and put into practice angles never dreamed of a decade earlier. Now, instead of always coasting at right-angles to the wave . . . the most skilled would often be seen erect on boards that their feet and balance guided at astonishing slants.[6]

Modern surfers had finally recovered some of the skill that greeted Captain Cook some 140 years earlier. Surfing, it seems, or rather the surfers themselves were back on their feet. For the next twenty years board construction increased, and the number of surfers grew to several hundred. All this time the sport remained primarily localized at Waikīkī. According to surfers of the 1920s, surfing was rare on outside islands or even around the rest of O'ahu. It wasn't until the late

1930s that Honoluluans began to "discover" good surfing spots on the other shores of their island—places like Mākaha, Makapu'u, and Paumalū (Sunset Beach), all of which had been surfed by early Hawaiians. During the thirties surfing was also reintroduced to Maui and Kaua'i by former Honolulu residents.

The Second World War interrupted the sport's expansion. But afterward interest was restimulated by a new association, The Waikīkī Surf Club. By 1947 the two original clubs had changed considerably. Hui Nalu had limited its activities almost solely to outrigger canoe-racing. The Outrigger Canoe Club was now an exclusive establishment with a wide range of social and athletic interests. The reasons behind the Waikīkī Surf Club, then, were similar to those that had originally spurred the early clubs. Its purpose was to promote surfing as well as other Hawaiian water sports. It provided board lockers and clothes-changing facilities near the beach for anyone who could pay the small initiation fee and monthly dues. The need for

such a club was soon apparent. Under the leadership of John Lind it gained six hundred members in ninety days. Since then several more surf clubs have appeared at Waikīkī. The Outrigger is still the oldest

SURF CANOES AND SURFERS AT WAIKĪKĪ BEACH, C. 1910–1915. PHOTO COURTESY HAWAIIAN HISTORICAL SOCIETY.

and largest, but all are important in supporting the sport and providing organizations for a steadily growing body of surfers. Still, the sport is indebted to the Waikīkī Surf Club for much of its post-war growth. The club initiated and sponsored several surfing and aquatic events that have stimulated public interest and healthy competition: the Diamond Head Surfboard Paddling Championships, the grueling Moloka'i-O'ahu Outrigger Canoe Race, the Makapu'u Bodysurfing Championships, and the now-famous International Surfing Championships at Mākaha, O'ahu.

Another factor important to post-war growth was the migration to Hawai'i of surfers from California. It actually began in the 1920s when Californians like Tom Blake and Sam Reid journeyed into the Pacific to taste the fabled waves. But such journeys were few compared to the influx that began in the late 1940s and continues to this day. The sport had grown rapidly on the U.S. mainland ever since 1907. The post-war years found Californians more eager than ever to tackle Hawai'i's surf. They tried Waikīkī first and generally were not impressed. But once they rode the great north swell at Mākaha, northwest of Waikīkī, the rush from California really began. Since 1949 many Californians, as if proving Jack London's prophesy, have taken up permanent residence in Hawai'i, to be on hand when the surf is running. Many others make the 2,500-mile trip annually to spend a month or so riding the towering fall and winter waves on O'ahu's north shore. This flow of Californians bringing new board designs and fresh riding techniques made a terrific impact on the Hawaiian sport. After the war, in fact, Hawaiian surfing was spurred by the combination of its enthusiastic internal growth with this stimulus from its nearest continental neighbor.

A SURFER RIDES THE WAVES WITH HIS DOG AT WAIKĪKĪ IN 1932. PHOTO COURTESTY BAKER COLLECTION, BISHOP MUSEUM, HONOLULU.

DEVELOPMENT OF THE SURFBOARD

The modern surfboard, for example, was developed through experiments in both places: Californians provided many of the ideas; Hawai'i provided ideas as well as the waves that challenged the board builders' ingenuity. The history of the board's evolution closely parallels the sport's revival. The two, in fact, depend on each other. As boards became more efficient and available, more people surfed; riding techniques improved. This in turn demanded better boards. At the lowest ebb some surfers had used any plank or scrap of wood they could find along the beach. Half a century later the same beaches were studded with trim, glistening, many-colored boards that brought to this ancient pastime the benefits of modern technology. To trace this development and the important relationship that grew between Hawai'i and California, we must return briefly to the turn of the century.

As surfing was being revived, the first twentieth-century boards were around six or seven feet long and resembled the old alaia boards except in their thickness and cross-sectional shape (see board A in fig.

THE HUI NALU SURF CLUB, INCLUDING DUKE KANANAMOKU AND SEVERAL OF HIS BROTHERS, C. 1920. PHOTO COURTESY HAWAI'I MARITIME CENTER.

6). They were two to three inches thick, flat on top, with a slightly convex bottom and rounded edges. The native woods, koa and wiliwili, were replaced by redwood, pine, and other imports. As a finish, marine varnish was used, rather than burnt kukui-nut juice. Although soon superseded, these short pioneer craft mark the beginning of the transition to modern boards, using the old alaia as a departure point. By contrast, in this period there were few attempts to duplicate the kingly olo. By 1907 these heavy planks were scarce at Waikīkī. Perhaps the last time a traditional olo caught an ocean swell was around 1915.

Another type of board, similar to the first alaia copy, appeared in 1910 (board B, fig. 6). It was slimmer and longer. Such boards were used for at least twenty years after their introduction. By 1926 the surfboard had grown another foot or two, and a pointed nose was popular (board C, fig. 6). Some builders were using alternating strips of laminated pine or redwood instead of one of several planks of the same wood. These boards combined the strength of pine with the

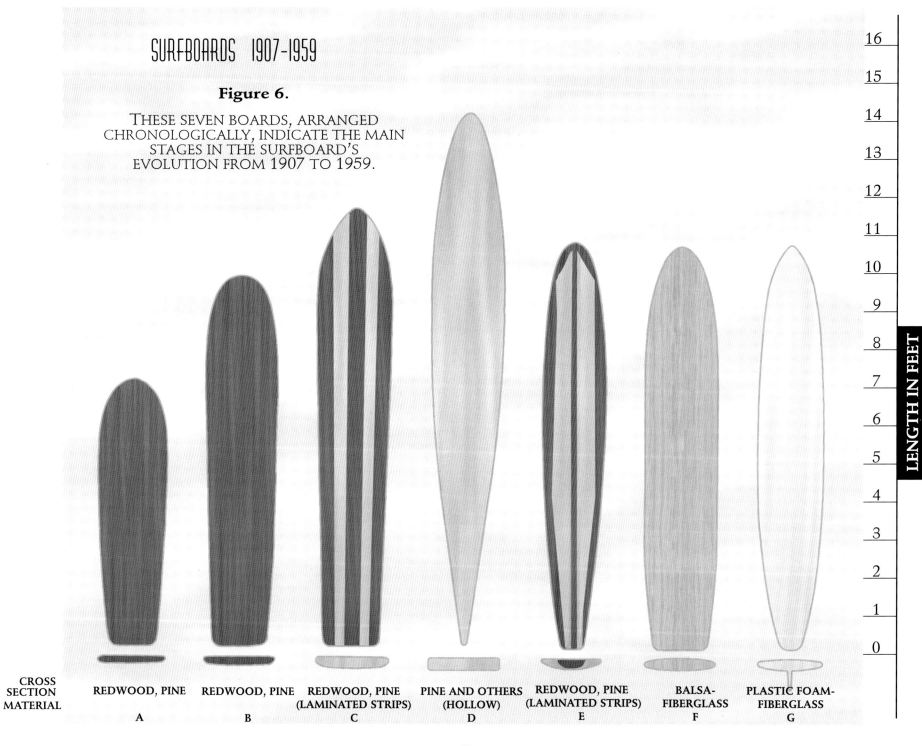

SURFBOARDS 1907-1959

Figure 6.

THESE SEVEN BOARDS, ARRANGED CHRONOLOGICALLY, INDICATE THE MAIN STAGES IN THE SURFBOARD'S EVOLUTION FROM 1907 TO 1959.

LENGTH IN FEET

16
15
14
13
12
11
10
9
8
7
6
5
4
3
2
1
0

CROSS SECTION MATERIAL

REDWOOD, PINE
A

REDWOOD, PINE
B

REDWOOD, PINE (LAMINATED STRIPS)
C

PINE AND OTHERS (HOLLOW)
D

REDWOOD, PINE (LAMINATED STRIPS)
E

BALSA-FIBERGLASS
F

PLASTIC FOAM-FIBERGLASS
G

light weight of redwood and were believed to be more functional as well as more attractive. About this time lightweight balsa boards were first tried but were dismissed as too light and fragile for practical use.

These first three designs all grew from the alaia shape common in early Hawai'i. In the 1930s an ambitious California surfer came along and began to experiment in another direction. Tom Blake wanted to build a fast-paddling, buoyant board comparable to the ancient olo. First he copied the examples in the Bishop Museum. His longest boards stretched sixteen feet, a foot shorter than the biggest surviving olo. They differed from the olo in that they were flat-decked, built of redwood, and hollow. They were excellent for paddling and also successful in the surf. Like the olo they were well adapted to the glossy rollers at Waikīkī. A surfer could catch a wave far out beyond the break, while the swell was still a gently, shore-rolling slope, and the board would slide easily along, whether the wave grew steep and broke or barely rose and flattened out again. From the performance of Blake's boards many otherwise unknown details of ancient olo technique could be estimated.

In 1935 Blake produced a lighter, point-tailed model (board D, fig. 6), built up of hollow compartments. Because of its ease in paddling and in catching waves, it became a favorite in Hawai'i and California, especially among novices, and it was used until the early 1950s. This was the end-product of Blake's experiments, however. His olo-inspired shapes led to no further development. Although big hollow boards dominated Hawaiian beaches for many years, by the 1960s they were seldom seen moving with an ocean swell and were found mainly along the beaches as standard lifesaving equipment. The surfboard's evolution continued from the solid, wide-tailed designs that preceded Blake's experiments.

When O'ahu surfers finally broke away from Waikīkī in the late 1930s and began riding the steep, fast-breaking waves on other parts of their island, they found their boards inadequate. As they caught these waves and turned to ride at an angle, often at the moment when the wave was steepest, the rider would lose control as his board slipped sideways or even tail-first into the wave's trough. Faced with such a frustrating and sometimes hazardous experience, surfers set about to remedy this "sliding tail." With some startling innovations John Kelly, a Honolulu surfer, partially solved the problem, produced a faster board, and pointed the way toward the functional big-surf boards of later years. With the exception of Blake's pin-tailed hollow boards, most boards still had parallel rails. Kelly narrowed the tail of a standard solid board, tapering its rails to produce what came to be known popularly as the "Island shape" (board E, fig. 6). This same basic deck plan is still used on boards shaped for speed. Kelly also rounded the bottom to make the sliding surface more convex, and he fashioned a narrow tail about six inches wide and slightly V-shaped in cross-section. The V tail acted as a keel that prevented sliding at the critical moment. But in solving one problem he created another: the V extended several feet along the bottom, and its keel effect sometimes made turning difficult. By slightly rounding the V tail, turning was easier, but if rounded too much, the keel effect was lost. Thus the V tail was a compromise, not a complete solution to the problem of stability and easy turning. Even so, with its revolutionary appearance in 1937, surfers could attempt larger, faster, and more exhilarating rides.

After World War II, southern California became a center for experimentation. Although authorities differ whether Tom Blake in Hawai'i or surfers in California first experimented with a skeg or tail fin, it appears that California innovators developed the skeg in its present form. This triangular fin, about six inches long and six inches

THOMAS EDWARD BLAKE, A "MAINLAND HAOLE" WHO SURFED FOR YEARS IN HAWAI'I, STANDS BEFORE SOME OF THE SURFBOARDS HE BUILT, 1935. THE ONE DIRECTLY BEHIND HIM IS MADE OF REDWOOD AND MEASURES 11 FEET LONG, 23 INCHES WIDE, AND 3 1/4 INCHES THICK. NEXT TO IT STANDS A RED CEDAR BOARD AT 12 FEET LONG; IT IS GOOD FOR FAST PADDLING. FOR BIG WAVES, THE THIRD— HOLLOW AND MEASURING 14 1/2 FEET BY 20 INCHES AND WEIGHING 120 POUNDS—WAS EASIER TO HANDLE THAN THE FOURTH, A REPRODUCTION OF THE ANCIENT HAWAIIAN RIDER. THE FIFTH IS A LIGHT, HOLLOW 16- FOOTER, AND THE LAST IS A TRAINING BOARD, SOLID AND HEAVY.

deep, keeps a board from side slipping on steep waves, or "sliding tail," as it is called.* Another innovation more securely attributed to California experimenters is covering balsa wood boards with fiberglass impregnated in plastic resin. During the 1930s and 1940s, attempts to make boards solely out of balsa wood failed; the light wood was too weak and porous. Covering balsa boards with fiberglass served both to strengthen and waterproof them. Other innovations credited to Californians during this period were the "scoop nose," which helps to keep a board from "submarining" nose-first as it drops into a wave; "rocker," bottom curvature from nose to tail; and a slightly rounded deck like those of the old alaia. This combination produced a faster, lighter, and more efficient surfboard that was immediately successful. The new design (board F, fig. 6) with skeg, fiberglassed balsa, and a graceful, streamlined shape reached Hawai'i in 1949, and just as had happened in California, it soon began to replace the older skegless solid and hollow boards.

Although surfers could now ride as no one had ridden before, they were still not satisfied. They probably never will be satisfied. Experiments on this basic modern design have continued. Board G (fig.6) is an example from the late 1950s of their continuing search for the "perfect board." The tail has narrowed again, the nose is more pointed, and the bottom camber is increased. This camber diminishes the danger of the board's nose digging into the wave. Not only the sleek design of this board distinguishes it from its predecessors, however; the materials do as well. Just as pine and redwood replaced indigenous woods in Hawai'i, so did balsa replace all other woods shaped in California for riding waves.

But as surfing expanded, balsa grew scarce and more expensive. California board builders searching for a new material came up with solidified plastic foam. The first foam boards appeared in the mid 1950s. Today, thousands of boards along the lines of board G are manufactured yearly in California factories devoted exclusively to the mass-production of foam boards. This plastic material, polyurethane, is lighter than balsa. In liquid form it is poured into a board-shaped mold where it hardens. The resulting "blank" is shaped, then reinforced and waterproofed with fiberglass and resin. Board G, then, while by no means universal or final in its design, is typical of this combination of technology with the demands of modern surfing in Hawai'i and California.

Numerous variations continue to appear, of course: experiments in tail width, nose pointage, thickness, camber, and skeg shape. Many changes are influenced by fashion, personal preference, or the search for novelty. Others genuinely contribute to the advance of board design. Much experimentation, for example, has resulted from a general division on modern design that began to be evident in the early 1950s. There is, on one hand, the highly maneuverable "hotdog" board, and on the other, the faster but hard-turning "gun" board. The gun boards, characterized by a longitudinal flatness somewhat analogous to that of the early olos, allow the greater speed necessary on the giant waves of O'ahu's north shore. The hotdog board, with its curved bottom and rounded edges, allows fast turns and fancy performance in small and medium surf, but at the price of reduced speed due to contour drag. Many have attempted to combine in a single board the gun's speed and drive with the hotdog's sensitive mobility.

*Could it be that the convex cross-section of the old alaia and olo boards kept riders from "sliding tail" when they surfed diagonally (lala) across the face of steep waves at such formidable surf spots as Paumalū and Kekaiomāmala?

The search for the perfect board is by no means over. Even so, a great deal has been achieved. Surfers now have boards that are light, buoyant, easy to paddle, and generally more manageable than boards have ever been before. The planks and straight-off sloping rides of 1900 have been replaced by the sleek vehicles that now can whirl and swerve, curving their white wakes in the fastest-breaking surf, or can streak, with fiberglass gleaming, across walls five times as high as the rider.

SURFING IN MODERN HAWAI'I

[Note: the perspective here is from the mid 1960s. As mentioned in the Foreword, we hope this chapter and the next can be read as a view of the sport at a specific period in its ongoing evolution.]

The comparison of today's board with its ancestor of sixty years ago is no less striking than to compare the same modern board with an old olo or alaia resting in the Bishop Museum. Plastic foam and koa are worlds apart, in the same way that surfing today is as different from the early pastime as Americanized Hawai'i is from the traditional social order of the eighteenth century. Some things never change, of course. The waves, for instance, break now much as they did when Cook arrived. A sandbar may have shifted; more coral may have encrusted a reef; a modern wharf or breakwater may now divert a particular swell. Yet the winds, the currents, the howling storm centers, the tropical sun, and the shape of the ocean floor have remained much the same through the centuries. The relationship among the three basic elements of wave, board, and surfer is also essentially the same. And there are other similarities. In many ways, the modern sport is clearly descended from the ancient pastime. But as the elaborate character of early surfing almost disappeared, a new and multifaceted surfing world emerged—a world that certainly would confound Naihe, the champion of Ka'ū, or Kahikilani, Kaua'i's surfing prince.

Let us begin with a look at the surfers themselves. The surfboard's refinement has tremendously influenced the sport's popularity in Hawai'i, as well as around the world. For the aficionado it is now more exciting and challenging; for the beginner it is easier and quicker to learn. Thus more are drawn to it, and more remain once they catch on. The improved board is one of the principal reasons surfing in Hawai'i has blossomed from a little-known amusement practiced by a few to a major recreation once again. Although probably there are still fewer surfers now than in former times, today in Hawai'i several thousands regularly take to the surf. Hawaiians still dominate the sport, but they now share the waves with all those who call the islands home—Haole, Japanese, Chinese, Filipino, and others—as well as with the multitude of visitors, whether they be awkward learners or hardy pros. In former times all ages surfed, with men and women equally adept. This is still true to some extent. Today some men surf into their sixties. But most of Hawai'i's surfers are teenage boys or men in their twenties; this seems to be the age group with the leisure and inclination to pursue a sport that takes both time and energy. And compared to former times, Hawai'i's female surfing population is still small and vastly outnumbered. Yet among the girls and women who ride waves, there are several who compete in the annual Mākaha Championships. Like their Polynesian forebears, they are strong and capable of keeping pace with the men.

Today the majority of Hawai'i's surfers live and pursue their sport on O'ahu. This twenty-by-forty-mile chunk of sand, soil, and green mountains remains the hub of surfing in the islands. In part, this is simply because O'ahu contains more than 80 percent of the state's population. But it is also true that the revival has yet to take hold in the other islands. Today most waves break riderless along the rugged lava coast of the big island of Hawai'i, and most of the old surfing

THE SIX KAHANAMOKU BROTHERS IN 1953 IN FRONT OF "PRINCESS," THE CANOE THAT BELONGED TO PRINCE KŪHIŌ. LEFT TO RIGHT (YOUNGEST TO OLDEST): SARGENT HIʻIKUA KAHANAMOKU, LOUIS KOʻOLIKO KAHANAMOKU, SAMUEL ALAPAʻI KAHANAMOKU, WILLIAM OKUʻU KAHANAMOKU, DAVID PIʻIKOI KAHANAMOKU, AND DUKE PAOA KAHANAMOKU. PHOTO COURTESY JO-ANNE KAHANAMOKU STERLING.

paddling surfer, leaving legs awash. In contrast, modern boards support the entire body; some surfers take advantage of this buoyancy to kneel when paddling out, a habit which probably originated in California to keep drier and warmer in cold water.

To be sure, contemporary surfers still emphasize the ancient technique of lala, angling across the wave front, and standing is the only acceptable way to ride. Yet they have probably gone beyond ancient precedents in their emphasis on maneuvering. From nineteenth-century reports, it appears that most surfers were content to paddle, catch the wave, stand up, and then speed along the wave front in one direction. New boards and modern impatience have changed this. As it rises ready to break, every wave is a fresh challenge, and even if through long experience a surfer is familiar with the break, he or she never knows exactly what will happen until it happens. At the same time, waves that break in the same place are similar enough to give the rider something to count on. An experienced surfer can thus play a wave: speed up, slow down, swerve, change direction, ride in the trough or shoot along its thin crest; turn to the left by shifting right foot behind left and bearing down; swerve to the right by moving the right foot over to the right edge and leaning into the wave; stall by stepping back on the board; and speed up by walking to the nose. As if taunting a rival, a surfer tempts the edge of rolling water until nearly devoured by it, then suddenly, with quick footwork, the board shoots across the water wall, momentarily out of danger, until the gleeful surfer cuts deftly back to tempt again.

THE CAPITAL

One of the most important links between modern surfing and its Hawaiian past—as well as the most obvious evidence of the changes that separate the two—is surfing's so-called capital: Waikīkī. A vital surfing area for commoners and chiefs in early times, Waikīkī was the seat of the revival in this century; and today, although greatly altered since Pīkoi risked his life on a chiefess's wave, this narrow strip of hot sand and the broad blue-green lagoon has remained the core of the sport's activity. Better and faster waves break on other beaches around Oʻahu, and the peak of Hawaiʻi's surfing year—the Mākaha Championships—takes place in "the country" far from Honolulu. Yet it is at Waikīkī that local residents learn how to surf. It is to Waikīkī that almost every overseas surfer goes upon arriving in the islands. And it is from Waikīkī that these same surfers radiate to other Oʻahu surfing spots. There, at the edge of Honolulu and beneath the volcanic furrows of Diamond Head, many of the surfing clubs have their headquarters. There, as nowhere else in the world, one can sit on white sand in the tropical sun and watch board-surfers, body-surfers, and fully crewed outrigger canoes all riding waves at the same time. The world's most photographed bay boasts some twelve separate surfing areas, from "First Break," which is the farthest offshore and breaks only a few times each year in a large swell, to "Canoes," whose wide blue slopes are ideal for the big outriggers and for beginning surfers.

There also one finds the famous "beach boys," mostly Hawaiians who by taking advantage of the commercial possibilities have made surfing and the beach their profession. Generally sun browned and well built, they are among the best surfers in the islands and frequently place high in the big contests. When not surfing, they run private concessions on the sand or work for larger concerns like the Waikīkī Beach hotels. They give surfboard lessons, ukulele lessons, offer boards and canoes for rent, and take loads of tourists in outriggers to slide the easy swells. These handy concessions, especially the board rentals, have proved to be another major factor in surfing's rapid post-war growth in Hawai'i. Located within a few yards of breaking surf, they provide a chance for tourists to give the waves a try and a chance for casual surfers who don't own boards to ride conveniently. Many a surfer got started on a rental board at Waikīkī.

It is no surprise that early Hawaiians chose this area as a favorite place to live and surf. There, the first day of winter is usually like the first day of summer or the first day of spring. The sky is almost always deep blue, with soft fat clouds easing down from the mountains over the hotel tops and out to sea. However, because the weather is so irresistible, because there are so many waves to ride and so many boards on which to ride them, Waikīkī has become the world's most crowded—or should we say, most popular—surfing area. On weekends it is not unusual to count three hundred or more surfers and hopefuls in the water at one time. During those few days of the year when Waikīkī surf gets big—ten to fifteen feet and sometimes larger at "First Break"—the inner water is less congested. But such days are rare. With Hawai'i's booming tourist trade, cheaper transportation rates, and more surfers from all parts of the world visiting the islands each year, the already famous "log jam" gets thicker every season.

THE CHAMPIONS

At least once each year the crowd scene shifts some forty miles up the leeward coast of O'ahu to the mouth of a verdant valley called Mākaha. Thousands of spectators cover the beach to sit under blazing sun and watch top-flight surfers compete in the International Surfing Championships. Begun in 1953 this is now the world's largest event devoted exclusively to surf-riding.

Mākaha was chosen as the contest site because it provides some of Hawai'i's finest surf. Waves there break to the right, and on a big day the shoulder of white water moving across a shore-rolling twelve-footer may hold up for several hundred yards. Because of its leeward location the beach is usually hot and dry. The only variable is the surf itself. Consequently, the championships are held on two weekends in late November or early December, when a good north swell is most likely.

The championship spectacle itself recalls the old public surfing contests and the grand sporting events at long ago Makahiki festivals. The fantastic wagers that appealed so much to the early noblemen, of course, are no longer the focus of onshore activity. But with multitudes filling the beach (often ten thousand or more) carrying food and drink for the day's outing, with scores of boards in and out of the water, and with glistening brown bodies racing shoreward then paddling back swiftly to bob and wait beyond the breaker line, it doesn't seem far removed from what must have happened two hundred years ago.

Also reminiscent of the old days is the scoring system devised by the contest originators. Buoys are used for markers, just as in the ancient contests. One buoy is anchored close to shore to mark the finish line; others are anchored progressively farther from shore, in line with the first. The farther out a wave is caught, judged by the buoy opposite which the surfer begins a ride, the more points are possible for that ride. To receive points a surfer must ride, standing on his board, past the inside buoy. Contestants compete in four divisions: Senior Men, Junior Men (seventeen years and under), Women, and Mixed Tandem. Entries may total 150 surfers or more, with several heats in each division. Because the heats in each event last an hour, the contest is one of stamina and paddling speed as well as riding ability. The winner is the one who can paddle fast, catch the most waves, handle them well, and ride them past the inside buoy.

Championship competition is keen. On a hot day with a heavy surf and with walls of "soup" to push through, it can be grueling.

Some surfers train for weeks ahead of time, paddling, swimming, and perfecting footwork. The winners are well rewarded. In addition to earning handcarved wood trophies or traditional Hawaiian calabashes, they have the thrill of riding Mākaha's surf, plus the glory of performing before an enthusiastic surf-educated audience. For the winners, the crowds, and surfing itself, the annual International Championships is the climax of each surfing year and the surest proof of the sport's popular revival.

What happens at Mākaha and a few places like it during the rest of the fall and winter, on days when the north swell is at its largest, is the surest proof of yet another dimension of surfing's modern growth in Hawai'i. While boards have improved, and while the sport itself attracts more and more hopefuls each day, the hardiest of experienced surfers have continued to learn about the ocean and to experiment with what a board can do on a wave, thus improving their capacity to grapple with the surf. Now, they paddle out among waves that literally shake the earth when they break. The size of waves such surfers attempt depends upon several factors; among them are board design, physical endurance under water as well as on the surface, and the sheer strength to paddle through the currents and heavy sea that inevitably accompany large waves. Some say that big-wave surfers have reached their limit. Others say better boards and more experience will make ever-bigger waves manageable. Whether the biggest wave has yet been ridden or not, winter surf on O'ahu's north shore, at places like Paumalū, Waimea, or Laniākea, already provides one of the most daring sights one will ever see on the edge of the ocean: a nearly naked surfer dwarfed by a thirty-foot ocean swell, like a seahorse caught in the gaping jaws of a sperm whale, yet riding the wave for the final seconds of its lonely life, drawing a foamy finger across its green and empty face.

The feats of such surfers have become part of modern legend. Already there are tales told on beaches of the heroes and the highest waves. Surfing is a sport that breeds big stories. The adventures of Kelea, Māmala, Hauailiki, and Umi-a-līloa are among those that survived in Hawaiian legend, and the list of legends keeps growing. From the nineteenth century, for example, comes the story of Holoua, a man of Kaua'i who was washed out to sea by a tsunami with his house and all his belongings. Tsunami waves come in sets, and according to the story, the next one was a fifty-footer. As it swelled behind him, Holoua ripped a plank from the side of his house and rode the mountain of water back to shore. In more recent times, even before the north shore was rediscovered, modern myths began—blends of fact and fiction—that have since circulated by word of mouth from beach to beach. At Waikīkī, it is said, two early-twentieth-century surfers reputedly caught one wave so far out from shore that when one angled to the right and the other angled to the left, they met a short time later at Kahuku Point, the island's northernmost tip, on the opposite side of O'ahu.

Such stories differ from more recent tales of giant surf, perhaps because the tales inspired by the north swell, although sometimes fantastic, are still new enough to be true. There are tales of waves so ferocious that balsa and foam boards have been caught and shattered, not by rocks, but by sheer crashing power. Others tell of rides so fast that whole boards have been denuded when the moving water found a tiny rip in the fiberglass cover and flayed the board clean in an instant. One hears of surfers who can barely swim, who can only dogpaddle, yet face the largest waves; of men who can swim for twenty hours, claiming to have no qualms about the most tempestuous boil; and of strange communities where surf-hungry Californians huddle together in battered panel trucks, parking where the "heavies" break, riding waves from dawn until dark, purposely denying themselves the fabled pleasures of the tropics, preferring a forced austerity—like ascetics on a pilgrimage to the Himalayas.

One story tells of three surfers riding giant waves at Paumalū who were caught half a mile offshore in rising surf that was suddenly too big to ride. The coast was closing out, and there was no order in the ugly sea that surrounded them, that broke before and behind them. They fought currents and walls of white water on their tiny chips of balsa, and it was only through knowledge of local reefs and channels that they finally made it to shore, nearly in a state of collapse from their hours of chaotic paddling.

On another day three men were surfing at Mākaha, with waves humping to fifteen feet or a little more, when a swell loomed up such as none of them had seen before. Frantically they began to paddle for the horizon, hoping to reach the wave and paddle over the top before it crushed them. As it grew they realized it was nearly thirty feet high and they could never get into the right position to take off and ride it—even if they wanted to. Two of the surfers let their boards go at the last moment and dove for the bottom. The third, a faster paddler, was farther out and continued pulling with all his strength, paddling right up the towering face. When he neared the top his board was pointing almost skyward, and just as the wave crest

IN 1868—SO THE LEGEND GOES—HOLOUA RODE A TIDAL WAVE BACK TO SHORE ON A PLANK HE TORE FROM HIS HOUSE. PAINTING BY C. P. CATHCART; PHOTO COURTESY HAWAI'I MARITIME CENTER, HONOLULU.

feathered to tumble over him, he scrambled to the board's nose and leaped screaming over the top. The others were nearly drowned, and his board was later found on shore in pieces.

Such stories suggest the skill, stamina, courage, and craftsmanship required on the frontiers of modern Hawaiian surfing. With this perspective it is indeed strange to glance once again around the rest of Polynesia, where we find that without exception in every other island group surf sports are still a children's pastime, if practiced at all. Among the Tahitians and Māori of Aotearoa, whose islands were former surfing centers, the sport is, as we have seen, virtually dead. By comparison, the sport's status in modern Hawai'i is even more remarkable. All three societies—Hawaiian, Tahitian, and Māori—felt the brutal impact of disrupting Western influence. In Hawai'i, however, though surfing declined seriously, a tradition of recreational surf-swimming lived on. The lack of this in Tahiti and Aotearoa may have prevented a revival of surfing among the southern islanders themselves. Moreover, since Hawaiian surfing was more elaborate and socially important, it may have survived longer into the nineteenth century and thus have offered a more substantial sport to attract new Haole. The erect riding position probably had more appeal than whatever wave-riding pastimes survived in Tahiti or Aotearoa. At any rate, in neither area did European residents take an interest in the sport in time to stop its disappearance. Environmentally, of course, no islands can match Hawai'i's blend of location, climate, and wave shapes. The modern revival, then, seems indebted to the fortunate combination of three elements: favorable locations, an advanced form of the sport, and an enthusiastic group of Haole and modern Hawaiians who rekindled interest. Once the revival was under way, island residents of all races joined with Californians and other surfers to transform surfing's turn-of-the-century remnants into what we can once again call a "national pastime."

In another sense, though, surfing is more than mere pastime. A glistening Polynesian youth gliding gracefully on a surfboard has become a symbol of all the tropical pleasures Hawai'i has to offer the careworn Westerner. With Diamond Head as a backdrop, the beachboy guiding a canoe-load of laughing *mālihini* (newcomers) down the slope of a wave at Waikīkī has become the world's image of "The Paradise of the Pacific." When the old order died away in Hawai'i, much that made surfing significant died with it: the chiefly contests, surfing chants, gambling, board-building rituals, legends, vocabulary, and place names. The ancient complex of related activities never reappeared; the time and social climate that created them was gone forever. Yet in the twentieth century, much has grown up to replace all that. With clubs, championships, commercial importance, a colorful capital, mountainous waves to generate modern myths, and worldwide romantic symbolism, surfing has grown beyond the level of pastime to become, as it was in former days, an institution in modern Hawai'i.

MĀKAHA, MID 1950S. THIS IS ONE OF THE FIRST PHOTOGRAPHS OF BIG-WAVE SURFING THAT AWAKENED WORLDWIDE INTEREST IN SURFING IN HAWAI'I.
PHOTO COURTESY HAWAI'I VISITORS BUREAU.

Surfers in front of the Moana Hotel, Waikīkī, mid 1920s. Left to right: Kealoha, Samuel Alapaʻi Kahanamoku, David Piʻikoi Kahanamoku, Hiram Anahu, Kim Wai, and William Okuʻu Kahanamoku. The Kahanamokus were brothers of the famous Duke Kahanamoku.

CHAPTER SIX

Surfing Goes International

This serene Pacific . . . rolls the midmost waters of the world, the Indian Ocean and the Atlantic being but its arms . . . this mysterious, divine Pacific zones the world's whole bulk about; makes all coasts one bay to it; seems the tide-beating heart of earth.

—HERMAN MELVILLE

If twentieth-century surfing had never left the beaches where it long ago had flourished, its rebirth would still be unique in Hawaiian history. Few aspects of the ancient culture survived into modern times. None can match this spectacular resurgence. But the story doesn't end in this necklace of islands. While their sport was growing at home, Hawaiians were out showing the rest of the world how to do it. Surfing became one of the rare features of early culture to thrive outside the islands themselves. By legend and example it spread to surfable seacoasts on five continents.

CALIFORNIA

Three Hawaiian princes introduced surfing to California. Jonah Kūhiō Kalaniana'ole* and his brothers, David and Edward, were nephews of Queen Kapi'olani, queen to Hawai'i's last king, David Kalākaua. In 1885, while attending St. Matthew's Military School in San Mateo, California, they visited nearby Santa Cruz. That summer, before astonished crowds, they surfed off the mouth of the San Lorenzo River, riding long boards that had been milled from local redwood logs. But the princes were ahead of their time: few Californians were yet ready to follow their example.

In 1907, George Freeth, the ace Hawaiian surfer, brought this unfamiliar sport to southern California. Freeth's visit was a promotion sponsored by the Redondo–Los Angeles Railroad Company to introduce water sports to a public whose interest in ocean recreation was blossoming. He gave wave-riding demonstrations, and like Ford at Waikīkī, he offered surfing classes to youngsters. Freeth performed feats in the surf that have since become legendary. During the Santa Monica Bay storm of December 1908, for example, he single-handedly rescued seven Japanese fishermen in three successive trips through cold, crushing waves, for which he received a Carnegie Medal.

About the time of Freeth's arrival, Jack London's article on "A Royal Sport" was published nationally and gave the new California sport a boost. Five years later Duke Paoa Kahanamoku came to southern California on his way to the 1912 Olympics, where he won a gold medal in swimming in the 100–meter freestyle. With his redwood board he astounded beach crowds at such now-famous surf spots as Santa Monica and Corona del Mar. At the time Duke was one of the world's fastest swimmers and a leading Waikīkī surfer; he is still known today as the grandfather of modern Hawaiian surfing.** (One of his

---

* Prince Kūhiō later became Hawai'i's delegate to Congress after the United States annexed the islands.
** Duke died in 1968. He was named for his father who had been given the first name of Duke to commemorate the visit of the Duke of Edinburgh to Hawai'i.

early boards, with his name across the bow, is preserved in the Bishop Museum.) Duke's first California trip greatly encouraged the growing body of surfers. Where surf-swimming had been popular, men and boys began using boards. Clubs sprang up along the coast. With all sizes of ridable surf rolling in from the north and south Pacific, with innumerable hot, sandy beaches stretching along its curving coastline, and with a new and growing tradition of outdoor living, California was a "natural."

After the inspiration of the three Hawaiian princes, Freeth, and Kahanamoku, California surfing followed an independent course. Board fashions in the early years were dictated from Hawai'i, and a few Californians visited the islands to surf. But even though the waves they rode swelled from the same ocean, surfers in Los Angeles and Honolulu were separated by some 2,500 miles of water, and the mainland sport developed parallel to, but for the most part, independently of Hawai'i.

By 1928 it was popular enough for Tom Blake to organize the Pacific Coast Surfriding Championships at Corona del Mar. Top surfers competed for the Tom Blake Trophy eight times between 1928 and 1941, until the Second World War discontinued the event. The great boom in California began after the war with the development of the balsa board. As more of these easier-to-handle boards appeared, more and more ocean-minded Californians took up the sport. High school and college students especially adopted it as their pastime. The demand prompted seasoned surfers to go into business, and board-building concessions sprouted in beach towns. For some, board-building became a profession. The plastic-foam boards and the factories that make them soon transformed the profession into an industry that produced tens of thousands of new boards annually. California became the world's board-building center. Prices ranged from eighty dol-

THREE HAWAIIAN PRINCES—JONAH KŪHIŌ KALANIANA'OLE, DAVID KAWĀNANAKOA, AND EDWARD KELI'IAHONUI—SURFED AT SANTA CRUZ, CALIFORNIA, IN 1885 WHILE THEY WERE STUDENTS AT A NEARBY MILITARY ACADEMY. THE THREE WERE BROTHERS, BUT EACH HAD BEEN GIVEN A DIFFERENT LAST NAME RECALLING A DISTINGUISHED ANCESTOR. PHOTO COURTESY BISHOP MUSEUM.

GEORGE FREETH, WHO INTRODUCED SURFING TO SOUTHERN CALIFORNIA, IS SEEN HERE IN 1909 AS HE RIDES A WAVE STRAIGHT-OFF AT REDONDO BEACH, CALIFORNIA. PHOTO BY R. E. MATTESON OF HERMOSA BEACH, CALIFORNIA; COURTESY DR. JOHN H. BALL.

DUKE KAHANAMOKU, ON A POSTER FOR THE 1914 MID-PACIFIC CARNIVAL. PHOTO COURTESY BISHOP MUSEUM, HONOLULU.

lars for a molded but unshaped board to two hundred dollars for some custom-made "gun" boards.* Many of these are sold around the globe, but the greatest market is still California, where an estimated 150,000 surfers crowd its beaches in the summer.

Mass-production stimulated the California sport; so have the full-length surfing movies shown in halls and auditoriums up and down the state throughout the year. The first commercial attempt to capture the color and action of surfing was a film produced by Bud Browne, of California, in 1953. Since then dozens more have appeared to delight surf-happy audiences from San Francisco to San Diego and from Honolulu to Melbourne. The stars are always the surfers themselves, riding the best waves in California, Hawai'i, Australia, Peru, and elsewhere. As well as stimulating interest wherever they are shown, these films have greatly increased the numbers of California surfers who travel to Hawai'i to try their luck.

Most Californians, however, surf at home, inhabiting the five hundred miles of coastline between San Francisco and the Mexican border. On those beaches where the best waves break, cults and minor sub-cultures have developed with speech patterns, vocabulary, conformity of dress, and social attitudes all built around the riding of waves. For some, the thrill of rising surf becomes a consuming passion that dominates their life, usually during the late teens and early twenties, but sometimes into adulthood. Whether a pastime or a profession, however, surfing gets into one's blood, and it is contagious. On any spring or summer weekend thousands of cars, some new, some amazingly dilapidated, race to the coast with boards lashed to the roof. The crowds, in fact, have become so great that at some popular beaches the welter of boards is more hazardous than the crushing power of the waves themselves. San Onofre, for example, is a popular beach but only one among hundreds of surfing spots in southern California. Yet when a surfing club was organized there, membership had to be "limited" to five hundred.

During the fall and winter, when water is colder and the weather less favorable, the crowds thin out. Those who remain have the advantage of less congestion plus larger waves, generated by winter storms. Winter surfing, especially in northern California where water temperatures often drop to 48 degrees, has been boosted by the advent of the wetsuit, a skin-tight rubber garment that protects the surfer

*1966 prices. Today a custom board can cost from $350 to $900 or more.

from the aching cold of December waves. On a typical winter day on beaches around Monterey Bay south of San Francisco, it is not unusual to see four or five surfers streaking across an ominously gray wave, standing on their boards like black-suited aquanauts. In addition to warmth, the suit gives surfers more buoyancy if they lose their board and must swim for it through the pummeling frigidity of the north swell. In the past the spread of surfing has depended, to a large extent, on bearable water temperatures. This invention, however, seems to have conquered cold water, and it may well extend the frontiers of surfing into previously unexplorable places.

Today the home of balsa, plastic foam, and the wetsuit ranks second only to Hawai'i as a thriving surf center. The United States Surfing Association (USSA) was organized in southern California in 1961 and has its headquarters there. Embracing the U.S. Pacific coast, the eastern seaboard, and Hawai'i, the USSA is the first national organization devoted exclusively to the betterment of surfing and surfing conditions. Moreover, the West Coast Surfboard Championships inaugurated at Huntington Beach in 1959 now rival Mākaha in crowds and surfing prowess. Although the event is dominated by Californians, several Hawaiians have entered and placed highly. In fact, since the days of the surfing princes, Freeth, and Kahanamoku, many Hawaiians have tried the mainland's chilly waters. But Hawai'i still receives the finest swells that break anywhere; this attracted Californians there in the late 1940s to begin the big migration and finally joined these two separate but related surfing movements. The result, of course, has been a mutual improvement in board-building and wave-riding technique.

As Hawai'i's closest continental neighbor and blessed with a good surfing environment, California was an obvious place for the reviving sport to flourish as it began its global spread.

AUSTRALIA

During the time of the revival in Hawai'i and the new movement in California, another world of surfers was coming to life down below the equator. As far back as the 1880s Australians, taught by a Pacific islander known as "Tommy Tanna," had learned to body-surf. Soon after the turn of the century, tales of Hawaiian surfing with boards traveled four thousand miles down the Pacific to reach Australia's beaches. Stimulated by this exciting notion, several body-surfers around Sydney tried to fashion their own boards. With only stories to guide them, however, their crude planks and unskilled riding attempts failed. Even a surfboard imported from Hawai'i in 1912 proved impossible to ride and eventually became an ironing board.

DUKE KAHANAMOKU, C. 1915.
PHOTO COURTESY BISHOP MUSEUM, HONOLULU.

Australian surfers needed an example, and they soon had one. In 1915 the indefatigable Duke Kahanamoku arrived to give swimming exhibitions. While there he built a board from local woods and finally gave the Australians a firsthand look at Hawaiian surfing. That was all they needed. After Duke's demonstrations, it began to spread in Australia as much as it did in California, but with a major difference.

Immediately the sport was integrated with a spirited organization soon to be called the Surf Life Saving Association of Australia (SLSA). Begun in 1907 it was formed primarily in the interest of water safety for surf-swimmers and bathers on the beaches of eastern Australia. A tradition of surf-swimming has, in most areas, preceded the successful arrival of surfing, and this was probably most true of Australia. By 1906 several clubs had been formed to protect beach-goers from hazards such as sharks, currents, and the large waves typical of Australia's coastline. These clubs banded together in 1907. When Kahanamoku arrived in 1915, the new movement was already an institution; the first Surf Lifesaving Carnival had been held near Sydney the previous year. The new sport of surf-riding was obviously included in the scope of this organization.

This association with Surf Lifesaving has shaped the character of the sport in Australia. In both Hawai'i and California, clubs have been important in the sport's growth, but in Australia they have had a unique significance, since the clubs there concentrate on lifesaving activities together with a whole range of ocean sports; in addition to board-surfing and body-surfing, it includes boat-surfing as well as riding waves on an unusual device peculiar to Australia called the surf-ski. An average ski is built of plywood, maybe seventeen feet long, about two feet wide, and weighing some ninety pounds. The rider sits on the board with feet in deck stirrups and paddles for the wave with a double-bladed oar. Since 1937 the bulky surf-ski has been part of the SLSA's standard rescue equipment, but it is still a popular and uniquely Australian wave-riding device.

Each year the SLSA sponsors the famous Surf Lifesaving Carnival, an event that draws daily crowds of fifty thousand or more, who come to watch competition in swimming, lifesaving skills, and surfing. In 1956 teams from California and Hawai'i competed in the carnival. Among those representing Hawai'i were Peter Balding, Tom Zahn, Tom Moore, Tommy Shroeder, Harry Shaffer, and Danny De Rago. The Hawaiian team made the trip primarily to observe firsthand the Australians lifesaving methods. But they also brought with them their fiberglassed balsa boards and set the Australians on fire with the performance and maneuverability of these lightweight craft.

Previously most Australian surfers, if not riding surf-skis, were using the so-called "cigar boxes": hollow boards similar to Blake's olo copies of the 1930s, about twelve feet long and made of plywood, cedar or maple, and screwed or glued together. Since 1956, balsa and foam boards have taken over Australia's beaches, and surfers there are now adept at all the sweeps, stalls, and fancy footwork of Malibu and Honolulu.

Today the Land Down Under is fast catching up with California as a populous surfing center. But, like Hawai'i, its significance in the history of the sport involves more than local growth. Australia has been a secondary point from which surf-consciousness has spread around the world. As the idea of their surf-lifesaving methods has reached other British Commonwealth countries, surfing has gone with it, and the SLSA clubs have become convenient focal points for all beach activity.

AOTEAROA

As we have seen, the Māori greatly enjoyed canoe-surfing, bodyboard surfing, and body-surfing, known collectively as *whakarērere*. By the

DUKE KAHANAMOKU WITH A 1930S VERSION OF THE ANCIENT OLO BOARD. PHOTO COURTESY BISHOP MUSEUM, HONOLULU.

1930s, however, traditional surfing apparently had declined significantly in popularity. During that decade, Australian Surf Lifesavers introduced their revision of the sport with surf-skis and "cigar boxes." These ponderous boards caught on among new recruits to the sport, particularly in the warmer waters of Aotearoa's North Island. Surfing received a further boost in the late 1950s when Californians brought the first balsa boards to Aotearoa, and since then interest in the new equipment and riding skills has been growing rapidly.

SOUTH AFRICA

Surfing was nothing new in Aotearoa; neither is it anything new to Africa. But there are thousands of miles and evidently hundreds of years between the indigenous sport practiced by coastal peoples of Senegal, Ivory Coast, and Ghana and the Hawaiian-derived sport flourishing in South Africa today. Although West Africans may still ride the waves as their ancestors did in centuries past, their sport does not appear to be linked historically with surfing around the Cape of Good Hope. It was the Australian example, this time spanning the Indian Ocean, that introduced the sport there.

In the beginning South Africans had only a rough sketch of an early ski, brought back by a swimming coach from the 1938 Empire Games at Sydney. The Surf Life Saving movement was already established, and a local lifesaver named Fred Crocker followed the design and built the country's first surf-ski: twelve feet long with a boarded deck, flat bottom, and heavy enough that two men were needed to handle it in the surf. Schoolboy Junior Lifesavers, however, learned to ride it, and the unwieldy craft was used for surfing until after World War II. Improved surf-skis appeared after the war, and in the 1950s Australian hollow boards replaced some of the skis. Also in the early fifties the South Beach Surf Board Club was formed in Durban. More recently balsa and foam boards have arrived so that today South African surfers are mastering modern riding techniques on Indian Ocean swells.

ENGLAND

In 1953 the Surf Life Saving movement was established in England, and with the unique safety methods came the surfboard, surf-ski, and all the oceanic skills developed on Australia's beaches. With its time-honored reputation for fog, foul weather, and the frigid English Channel, England seems an unlikely spot for a traditionally warm weather sport like surfing. But the southwest coasts of Devon and Cornwall boast the mildest summer climates in the British Isles, and the warm gulf stream, rushing up from the Caribbean, passes so near that water temperatures sometimes approach 60 degrees. This southern coast, full of steep cliffs, sandy coves, and long, shimmering beaches, receives a regular North Atlantic swell and has been a favorite holiday area for beach-minded Britons.

Bodyboard surfing has been known there since the early years of this century. In 1953, Allan Kennedy, an Australian, established a Surf Lifesaving club in Bude, Cornwall, and thus the first surfing club in Europe. Since then, some twenty other clubs have joined, and, as usual, lifesaving and surfing go hand in hand. Many British surfers use Australian surf-skis, but some imported boards are also available.

Unlike Hawai'i, where there are twelve surfing months in every year, surfing is a summer sport in England, which isn't surprising. The main surfing areas—scattered between south Devon and Land's End—are in a latitude parallel to the Sakhalin Island off the coast of Siberia and farther north than the Great Wall of China. Ride a wave off the Cornish coast, and you'll watch it break on the northernmost surfing beaches in the world.

ISRAEL

Beyond the British Commonwealth and outside the California-Hawaii zone, several other areas of the world have been introduced to Hawaiian surfing. Among these is Israel. A former Honolulu resident, Dorian Poskowitz, moved to Israel and organized a club to promote the sport. Israel's surfing is unique because it depends more upon local wind waves generated in the eastern Mediterranean than ocean storm centers looked to by most surfers.

FRANCE

Surfing did not come to France via a visiting surfer but by the successful diffusion of an idea. At Biarritz on the Atlantic coast near Bayonne, close to the Spanish border, swimming enthusiasts first read about the sport and heard tales of its glamour and excitement. After examining published plans of surfboards and studying technique in books, they built their own boards and proceeded to teach themselves to surf. French surfers thus set a precedent in the surfing world. Since this imaginative beginning, new stimulation has come from Californian and Australian surfers visiting France to try the waves around the Bay of Biscay. In tribute to surfing's capital, the French have formed Le Club Waikiki at Biarritz, which has become the surfing center for western Europe.

PERU

On the west coast of South America the great Pacific ground swell licks and lashes beaches from Panama to Cape Horn. But the only area on this endless coastline where surfers are known to ride waves regularly is in Peru, off beaches near Lima. In the 1930s a Peruvian visitor to Hawai'i, Carlos Dogny, fell in love with the ancient sport. When he returned home from one of his several visits to Honolulu,

he brought a board with him, and Peruvians have been surfing ever since. Due to the country's economic conditions, participation has been limited to the wealthier class. Although surfboards cost no more there than elsewhere they are too expensive for the average Peruvian.

The young men of Peru's well-to-do class, already interested in beach recreations, quickly took up surfing and have continued to support it. Today Peruvian surfing is characterized by a luxury found nowhere else in the surfing world. Most surfers belong to the swank Club Waikiki on the beach at Miraflores, only fifteen minutes from Lima. It was founded in 1942 by Dogny and three other surfing Peruvians. Much like a yacht club in appearance, the club is equipped with fish ponds, gardens, a squash court for winter recreation, a kitchen, bar, and clothes-changing facilities. It also provides members with the services of "board-boys" who fetch and carry surfboards to and from the water.

The Club Waikiki members got a fresh stimulus in 1955. Peruvian surfing went international when the exchange began between Lima and Honolulu. In that year George Downing, the 1954 Hawaiian Champion, entered a surfing tournament in Peru; he was the first Hawaiian representative to do so. Just as Kahanamoku inspired Australians and Californians some forty years earlier, so Downing gave Peruvians their first look at Hawaiian skill in big surf. Peru's biggest surfing waves break some twenty-five miles down the coast from Miraflores and the Club Waikiki at a beach now called Kon Tiki. Peruvians had tried its *olas grandes* but with little success until Downing showed them how. In 1955, moreover, the first balsa boards appeared in Peru. With Downing's example and *la tabla malibu*, the Malibu board, the Peruvians took it from there. They are keen competitors. Later the same year two Club Waikiki surfers carried their Hawaiian-inspired Peruvian sport back to O'ahu when they attended the International Championships at Mākaha.

In 1956 Carlos Dogny traveled to compete at Mākaha. While there he was particularly impressed by the unusual spectacle of women in competition. In Peru it was strictly a man's game. First he invited the women of the Waikīkī Surf Club to attend a Peruvian meet the next year. Then he extended the invitation to the club as a whole, to send a team to compete in what is now known as the South American Championships. The Hawaiian team—three men and three women—made the trip and won several trophies. But more importantly they were "cultural ambassadors" of sorts, as eager Peruvians kept them busy demonstrating riding technique, shaping and finishing boards, and describing the Hawaiian sport in detail. Two years later, Peruvians were back on Oʻahu with a delegation of nine, who competed with some of Hawaiʻi's champion surfers and proved themselves capable on Oʻahu's waves. By maintaining this contact with the sport's modern center, Peruvian surfers obtained valuable experience and encouragement. The success of their Hawaiʻi–South American Championships has earned the Peruvians their place in a dynamic and expanding surfing world.

MĀKAHA, MID 1950S. PHOTO COURTESY HAWAI'I VISITORS BUREAU.

There is the shaking sea,
the running sea of Kou,
Fine is the breeze from the mountain.

Surfing, of course, is still on the move, largely because of the surfers themselves. Regardless of their nationality, background, or walk of life, whether they live permanently on the beach or far inland, they are happily addicted to their sport. They love the smell of the sea, the look of the sea, and the feel of being immersed in or even near the sea. If they cannot ride they will watch the ocean, wondering at the waste of waves rolling shoreward without a rider. Surfing captures one's body through the very speed and fury of the ocean, and few surfers ever get it out of their systems or ever want to. This is one reason why it has spread so far and so fast. At the time of this writing [1966], French surfers have just discovered good waves off the Seychelles in the Indian Ocean, clubs are sprouting along the eastern seaboard of the United States, and Californians are surfing in Japan, Venezuela, Uruguay, and other newly discovered spots around the globe. Europeans are riding regularly off the Jersey Islands in the English Channel, and Hawaiians, the originators of the sport, are still enjoying their ancestral pastime in the warm, surf-filled waters of their incomparable islands.

Some impatient surfers, frustrated by the ocean's unpredictability, have even devised a way to surf where there is no surf. By catching the wake of a power boat, southern Californians have ridden their boards for miles across an otherwise placid sea. Experiments conducted in Long Beach Harbor and in Cypress Gardens, Florida, revealed that behind a small boat traveling at eleven or twelve knots, a surfer can experience much of the exhilaration and can perform many of the turns and stalls possible in ocean surf. The surfer uses a tow-rope to pick up speed, then lets it go and skims forward, propelled by the push of the wake itself. Although this is but a flat-day substitute for those who love the feel of the ocean's pulse beneath their feet, boat-wake surfing has opened up new territory for the surfboard. It means, of course, that the sport can now spread back from the coasts into harbors, surfless bays, and landlocked dams. It means that before long we may have surfing clubs in Nebraska or along the shore of Lake Titicaca, high in the Andes.

With all that, however, no matter to what far-flung reef or inland lake the sport may travel, Hawai'i remains the mecca. No one yet has found a place to match its blend of balmy climate, comfortable water, favorable swells, and exotic beauty. And it still offers the greatest challenge in the waves themselves and as a meeting place for international competitors. Jonah Kūhiō Kalaniana'ole, George Freeth, and Duke Kahanamoku carried their sport to the edges of the Pacific. Today surfers everywhere look back to Hawai'i and save their money to travel there. In Biarritz and in Lima, they pay homage with names like Club Waikiki. The Peru-Hawai'i exchange, moreover, mirrors the attitude of the surfing world as a whole. In 1957 Dorian Paskowitz returned to represent Israel in the Mākaha Championships. Californians, as we have seen, arrive each year by the hundreds. And in 1958 two Californians, Peter Cole and Marge Calhoun, became the first non-Hawaiian residents to ride off with the Senior Men and Senior Women's trophies at Mākaha. In 1962 the contests became truly international when the young Australian Bernard "Midget" Farrelley was named men's champion.

Probably the most dramatic signal of Hawai'i's international magnetism comes from South Africa. In 1958 two young South Africans sailed 14,000 miles in a thirty-foot yawl just to try Hawai'i's famous waves. It took them ten months to sail from Cape Town to Honolulu by way of the Panama Canal. For one month, caught in the doldrums, they lived on coconuts and fish. Later, one man fell overboard and nearly lost his hand to a shark. When the pilgrimage was over and they finally docked in Honolulu, the skipper, Charles Kennedy of Durban, said, "It's the gospel truth. We made the voyage just to go surfing in Hawai'i!"

Is it not possible that the same sentiments were uttered perhaps eight hundred years ago by some travel-weary chief of Tahiti, stepping out of his double-hulled canoe at Waikīkī? Dissatisfied with the surfing situation at home, might he not have packed his board in the hold, rounded up his paddlers, and headed north from Tahiti to try Paumalū or Kalehuawehe? Hawaiian legends record at least one surfing trip from Kaua'i to O'ahu, and we have seen how a wandering chief who had sailed up from Tahiti was attracted to live and die near a famous Kaua'i surf. Who knows what unrecorded expeditions may have spanned the Pacific in search of Hawaiian waves. Such speculations can never be answered, of course. Whether other islanders made such trips or not, there is no doubt that Hawai'i was the seat of surfing skill in ancient Polynesia. Today, no matter where it goes, surfing is still the sport that Hawaiians developed and then gave to the world.

APPENDIX A

HAWAIIAN SURFING TERMS

These definitions of Hawaiian surfing terms include their bibliographic sources, using the following key:

A: Andrews, Lorrin, 1865

B: Beckwith, Martha, 1919

E: Emerson, Nathaniel B., 1909

F: Fornander, Abraham, 1916–1920

H: Hawaiian Ethnological Notes

I: Iʻi, John Papa, 1959

PE: Pukui, Mary Kawena, and Samuel Elbert, 1986

T: Thrum, 1896

ahua: any place inside where the surf first rises and breaks; *kūlana nalu* is where the surf rises and breaks again (T, p. 109)

alaia: a thin, broad surfboard good for fast-breaking surf, usually made from koa or breadfruit; also called *omo* (PE, p. 17); nine feet long (I, p. 135)

ale: wave, crest of a wave, billow; apparently used more for open ocean swells than waves breaking on a shore (PE, p. 19)

ʻale lauloa: a long and large wave (PE, p. 19)

heʻe: to slide, to surf (PE, p. 63)

heʻe nalu: to ride a surfboard; surfing; surf-rider; literally, wave-sliding (PE, p. 63)

heʻe puʻewai: to surf toward the mouth of a stream, or up a stream (PE, p. 63)

heʻe umauma: body-surfing; to body-surf (PE, p. 63)

heihei nalu: a surfboard race (H, vol. 1, p. 656)

honua nalu: the base of a breaker (PE, p. 80)

hoʻonalu: to form waves (PE, p. 260)

huia: an especially high wave formed by the meeting of two crests, characteristic of the surf of Kaipalaoa, Hawaiʻi; literally, joined (B, p. 627; PE, p. 86)

huki: to pull, as in paddling with hands, straining to pull the water back to catch a wave (PE, p. 87)

kaha: to surf; to body-surf (PE, p. 110)

kākala: the surf in which an *alaia* board is used; a curling wave (F, vol. 6, p. 206) *kīko'o*: a twelve-to-eighteen-foot-long surfboard that is good for surf that breaks roughly but is difficult to handle (I, p. 135; PE, p. 150)

kīoe: a small surfboard (PE, p. 153)

kīpapa: prone position on a surfboard; to surf prone (PE, p. 154); a style of riding (T, p. 110)

kūlana nalu: place where the waves swell up and the surfer paddles to catch them, usually at the primary break farthest outside (PE, p. 179)

lala: riding at an angle; diagonal surf (PE, p. 191; seaward side of a cresting wave; crest of a wave (T, p. 109, 112)

lauloa: a long wave or surf breaking from one end of the beach to the other; one of two types of surfing waves, the other being the *'ōhū*, which rises without breaking; the same as a *kākala* (T, p. 109; PE, p. 196)

lele wa'a: canoe-leaping; jumping off a canoe with a surfboard onto a wave (I, p. 133; PE, p. 202)

muku: the cresting section of the wave face as opposed to the *honua*, the base (A, p. 109; PE, p. 256)

nalu: a wave; surf; full of waves; to form waves (PE, p. 260)

nalu ha'i lala: wave that breaks diagonally (PE, p. 260)

nalu kua loloa: long wave (PE, p. 260)

nalu miki: receding wave (PE, p. 260)

nalu muku: broken section of a wave (PE, p. 260)

nalunalu: rough, of a sea with high waves; to form high waves (PE, p. 260)

nalu pū kī: wave that shoots high (PE, p. 260)

'ōhū: one of two types of waves ridden, the other being *lauloa*; a low wave that rises without breaking but is of sufficient strength to be ridden with a surfboard (A, p. 109; PE, p. 278)

olo: a very long, narrow, and very thick surfboard with a marked double-convex lenticular cross-section; said to be reserved for the chiefs only and to be good for riding a non-breaking wave (see *'ōhū*) (T, p. 109; PE, p. 285; I, p. 135)

omo: a type of surfboard the same as the *alaia* (PE, p. 288)

'onaulu loa: a wave of great length and endurance (PE, p. 288; E, p. 35)

ōnini: a kind of surfboard difficult to manage, used by experts (*rare*, PE, p. 289); a thick surfboard of wiliwili wood (H, vol. 1, p. 655)

'ōpu'u: a large surf, swell (PE, p. 293)

'ōwili: a thick surfboard of wiliwili wood (A, p. 165; PE, p. 295)

paha: a kind of surfboard (*rare*, PE, p. 299)

pākā: to surf, as with a canoe, board, or body; to skim, as a surfing canoe (PE, p. 304)

papa heʻe nalu: a surfboard; literally, a board [for] wave-sliding. *Hāʻawi papa heʻe nalu* is to give with the understanding that the object will be returned [surfboards were loaned rather than given away permanently] (PE, p. 317)

puʻua: a surfboard (*rare*, PE, p. 358)

APPENDIX B
"First Description of Surfing," by Lt. James King, 1778

After the death of Captain Cook at Kealakekua, King took command of the expedition, which included the task of making daily entries in the log. In Chapter Three we have quoted from the first published version, heavily edited, as it appeared in London. This appendix is from Lieutenant King's unedited log (reprinted in *The Voyage of the Resolution and Discovery*, by John C. Beaglehole, 1967).

But a diversion the most common is upon the Water, where there is a very great Sea, & surf breaking on the Shore. The Men sometimes 20 or 30 go without the Swell of the Surf, & lay themselves flat upon an oval piece of plank about their Size & breadth, they keep their legs close on top of it, & their Arms are us'd to guide the plank, they wait the time of the greatest Swell that sets on Shore, & altogether push forward with their Arms to keep on its top, it sends them in with a most astonishing Velocity, & the great art is to guide the plank so as always to keep it in a proper direction on the top of the Swell, & as it alters its direct^n. If the Swell drives him close to the rocks before he is overtaken by its break, he is much prais'd. On first seeing this very dangerous diversion I did not conceive it possible but that some of them must be dashed to mummy against the sharp rocks, but just before they reach the shore, if they are very near, they quit their plank, & dive under till the Surf is broke, when the piece of plank is sent many yards by the force of the Surf from the beach. The greatest number are generally overtaken by the break of the swell, the force of which they avoid, diving & swimming under the water out of its impulse. By such like excercises, these men may be said to be almost amphibious. The Women could swim off to the Ship, & continue half a day in the Water, & afterwards return. The above diversion is only intended as an amusement, not a tryal of Skill, & in a gentle swell that sets on must I conceive be very pleasant, at least they seem to feel a great pleasure in the motion which this Exercise gives.

APPENDIX C

"Hawaiian Surfing in the 1820s," by William Ellis, from his *Polynesian Researches*, Vol. 3, 1831

Ellis was a touring British missionary. His description of surfing off Waimanu (near Waipiʻo, on the north coast of Hawaiʻi Island) refers to riding boards which, in size, fell between bodyboards and surfboards and only allowed the most expert of riders to stand erect.

As we crossed the head of the bay, we saw a number of young persons swimming in the surf, which rolled with some violence on the rocky beach. To a spectator nothing can appear more daring, and sometimes alarming, than to see a number of persons splashing about among the waves of the sea as they dash on the shore; yet this is the most popular and delightful of the native sports.

There are perhaps no people more accustomed to the water than the islanders of the Pacific; they seem almost a race of amphibious beings. Familiar with the sea from their birth, they lose all dread of it, and seem nearly as much at home in the water as on dry land. There are few children who are not taken into the sea by their mothers the second or third day after birth, and many who can swim as soon as they can walk. The heat of the climate is, no doubt, one source of the gratification they find in this amusement, which is so universal, that it is scarcely possible to pass along the shore where there are many habitations near, and not see a number of children playing in the sea. Here they remain for hours together, and yet I never knew of but one child being drowned during the number of years I have resided in the islands. They have a variety of games, and gambol as fearlessly in the water as the children of a school do in their play-ground. . . . but the most general and frequent game is swimming in the surf. The higher the sea and the larger the waves, in their opinion the better the sport. On these occasions they use a board, which they call *papa hé náru* [*papa heʻe nalu*], (wave sliding-board,) generally five or six feet long, and rather more than a foot wide, sometimes flat, but more frequently slightly convex on both sides. It is usually made of the wood of the *erythrina*, stained quite black, and preserved with great care. After using, it is placed in the sun till perfectly dry, when it is rubbed-over with cocoa-nut oil, frequently wrapped in cloth, and suspended in some part of their dwelling-house. Sometimes they choose a place where the deep water reaches to the beach, but generally prefer a part where the rocks are ten or twenty feet under water, and extend to a distance from the shore, as the surf breaks more violently over these. When playing in these places, each individual takes his board, and, pushing it before him, swims perhaps a quarter of a mile or more out to sea. They do not attempt to go over the billows which roll towards the shore, but watch their approach, and dive under water, allowing the billow to pass over their heads. When they reach outside of the rocks, where the waves first break, they adjust themselves on one end of the board, lying flat on their faces, and watch the approach of the largest billow; they then poise themselves on its highest edge, and, paddling as it were with their hands and feet, ride on the crest of the wave, in the midst of the spray and the foam, till within a yard or two of the rocks or the shore; and when the observers would expect to see them dashed to pieces, they steer with great address between the rocks, or slide off their board in a moment, grasp it by the middle, and dive under water, while the wave rolls on, and breaks among the rocks with a roaring noise, the effect of which is greatly heightened by the shouts and laughter of the natives in the water. Those who are expert frequently change their position on the board, sometimes sitting and sometimes standing erect in the midst of the foam. The greatest address is necessary in order to keep on the edge of the wave: for if they get too far forward, they are sure to be overturned; and if they fall back, they are buried beneath the succeeding billow.

Occasionally they take a very light canoe; but this, though directed in the same manner as the board, is much more difficult to manage. Sometimes the greater part of the inhabitants of a village go out to this sport, when the wind blows fresh toward the shore, and spend the greater part of the day in the water. All ranks and ages appear equally fond of it. We have seen Karaimoku and Kakioeva, some of the highest chiefs in the island, both between fifty and sixty years of age, and large corpulent men, balancing themselves on their narrow board, or splashing about in the foam, with as much satisfaction as youths of sixteen. They frequently play at the mouth of a large river, where the strong current running into the sea, and the rolling of waves towards the shore, produce a degree of agitation between the water of the river and the sea that would be fatal to a European, however expert he might be; yet in this they delight: and when the king or queen, or any high chiefs, are playing, none of the common people are allowed to approach these places, lest they spoil their sport. The chiefs pride themselves much on excelling in some of the games of their country; hence Taumuarii [Kaumuali'i], the late king of Tauai [Kaua'i], was celebrated as the most expert swimmer in the surf, known in the islands. The only circumstance that ever mars their pleasure in this diversion is the approach of a shark. When this happens, though they sometimes fly in every direction, they frequently unite, set up a loud shout, and make so much splashing in the water, as to frighten him away. Their fear of them, however, is very great; and after a party return from this amusement, almost the first question they are asked is, "Were there any sharks?" The fondness of the natives for the water must strike any person visiting their islands: long before he goes on shore he will see them swimming around his ship; and few ships leave without being accompanied part of the way out of the harbour by the natives, sporting in the water; but to see fifty or a hundred persons riding on an immense billow, half immersed in spray and foam, for a distance of several hundreds of yards together, is one of the most novel and interesting sports a foreigner can witness in the islands.

APPENDIX D

Excerpt from *Roughing It,* by Mark Twain

In 1866 Mark Twain sailed from San Francisco to Honolulu and spent several months in the islands, while sending back regular reports to *The Sacramento Union*. This trip was later included in the first edition of his book of western and Pacific travels, *Roughing It* (American Publishing Company, 1872). While visiting the Kona coast on the island of Hawai'i, Twain tried surfing.

At noon, we hired a Kanaka* to take us down to the ancient ruins at Honaunau in his canoe—price two dollars—reasonable enough, for a sea voyage of eight miles, counting both ways.

The native canoe is an irresponsible looking contrivance. I cannot think of anything to liken it to but a boy's sled runner hollowed out, and that does not quite convey the correct idea. It is about fifteen feet long, high and pointed at both ends, is a foot and a half or two feet deep, and so narrow that if you wedged a fat man into it you might not get him out again. It sits on top of the water like a duck, but it has an outrigger and does not upset easily if you keep still. This outrigger is formed of two long bent sticks, like plow handles, which project from one side, and to their outer ends is bound a curved beam composed of an extremely light wood, which skims along the surface of the water and

thus saves you from an upset on that side, while the outrigger's weight is not so easily lifted as to make an upset on the other side a thing to be greatly feared. Still, until one gets used to sitting perched upon this knife-blade, he is apt to reason within himself that it would be more comfortable if there were just an outrigger or so on the other side also.

MARK TWAIN, 1870.
PHOTO COURTESY R. KENT RASMUSSEN.

I had the bow seat, and Billings sat amidships and faced the Kanaka, who occupied the stern of the craft and did the paddling. With the first stroke the trim shell of a thing shot out from the shore like an arrow. There was not much to see. While we were on the shallow water of the reef, it was pastime to look down into the limpid depths at the large bunches of branching coral— the unique shrubbery of the sea. We lost that, though, when we got out into the dead blue water of the deep. But we had the picture of the surf, then, dashing angrily against the crag-bound shore and sending a foam-

---

* Kanaka is Hawaiian for person or human being. In the nineteenth century it came to mean a "native person."

ing spray high into the air. There was interest in this beetling border, too, for it was honey-combed with quaint caves and arches and tunnels, and had a rude semblance of the dilapidated architecture of ruined keeps and castles rising out of the restless sea. When this novelty ceased to be a novelty, we turned our eyes shoreward and gazed at the long mountain with its rich green forests stretching up into the curtaining clouds, and at the specks of houses in the rearward distance and the diminished schooner riding sleepily at anchor. And when these grew tiresome we dashed boldly into the midst of a school of huge, beastly porpoises engaged at their eternal game of arching over a wave and disappearing, and then doing it over again and keeping it up—always circling over, in that way, like so many well-submerged wheels. But the porpoises wheeled themselves away, and then we were thrown up on our own resources. It did not take many minutes to discover that the sun was blazing like a bonfire, and that the weather was of a melting temperature. It had a drowsing effect, too.

In one place we came upon a large company of naked natives, of both sexes and all ages, amusing themselves with the national pastime of surf-bathing. Each heathen would paddle three or four hundred yards out to sea, (taking a short board with him), then face the shore and wait for a particularly prodigious billow to come along; at the right moment he would fling his board upon its foamy crest and himself upon the board,

and here he would come whizzing by like a bombshell! It did not seem that a lightning express train could shoot along at a more hair-lifting speed. I tried surf-bathing once, subsequently, but made a failure of it. I got the board placed right, and at the right moment, too; but missed the connection myself. The board struck the shore in three-quarters of a second, without any cargo, and I struck the bottom about the same time, with a couple of barrels of water in me. None but natives ever master the art of surf-bathing thoroughly.

APPENDIX E

"Hawaiian Surf Riding," from *Thrum's Annual 1896*

For decades Thomas G. Thrum's *Hawaiian Almanac and Annual* was a basic source of island information and lore. The edition for 1896 contained one of the earliest accounts of surf-riding as conveyed by a native Hawaiian. According to Thrum, it was "prepared for the *Annual* by a native of the Kona district of Hawaii, familiar with the sport," and "N. K. Nakuina, himself no stranger to the sport in earlier days," assisted in the translation.

Surf riding was one of the favorite Hawaiian sports, in which chiefs, men, women and youth, took a lively interest. Much valuable time was spent by them in this practice throughout the day. Necessary work for the maintenance of the family, such as farming, fishing, mat and kapa [bark cloth] making, and such other household duties required of them and needing attention, by either head of the family, was often neglected for the prosecution of the sport. Betting was made an accompaniment thereof, both by the chiefs and the common people, as was done in all other games, such as wrestling, foot racing, quoits, checkers, holua, and several other known only to the old Hawaiians. Canoes, nets, lines, kapas, swine, poultry and all other property were staked, and in some instances life itself was put up as wagers, the property changing hands, and personal liberty, or even life itself, sacrificed according to the outcome of the match, the winners carrying off their riches and the losers and their families passing to a life of poverty or servitude.

TREES AND MODE OF CUTTING

There were only three kinds of trees known to be used for making boards for surf riding, viz.: the wiliwili (*Erythrina monosperma*), ulu or breadfruit (*Artocarpus incisa*), and koa (*Acacia koa*).

The uninitiated were naturally careless, or indifferent as to the method of cutting the chosen tree; but among those who desired success upon their labors the following rites were carefully observed.

Upon the selection of a suitable tree, a red fish called kumu was first procured, which was placed at its trunk. The tree was then cut down, after which a hole was dug at its root and the fish placed therein, with a prayer, as an offering in payment therefor. After this ceremony was performed, then the tree trunk was chipped away from each side until reduced to a board approximately of the dimensions desired, when it was pulled down to the beach and placed in the *halau* (canoe house) or other suitable place convenient for its finishing work.

FINISHING PROCESS

Coral of the corrugated variety termed *pohaku puna*, which could be gathered in abundance along the sea beach, and a rough kind of stone called *oahi* were commonly used articles for reducing and smoothing the rough surfaces of the board until all marks of the stone adze were obliterated. As a finishing stain the root of the ti plant (*Cordyline terminalis*), called *mole ki*, or the pounded bark of the kukui (*Aleurites moluccana*), called *hili*, was the mordant used for a paint made with the soot of burned kukui nuts. This furnished a durable, glossy black finish, far preferable to that made with the ashes of burned cane leaves, or amau fern, which had neither body nor gloss.

Before using the board there were other rites or ceremonies to be performed, for its dedication. As before, these were disregarded by the common people, but among those who followed the making of surf boards as a trade, they were religiously observed.

There are two kinds of boards for surf riding, one called the *olo* and the other the *a-la-ia*, known also as *omo*. The olo was made of wiliwili—a very light buoyant wood—some three fathoms long, two to three feet wide, and from six to eight inches thick along the middle of the board, lengthwise, but rounding toward the edges on both upper and lower sides. It is well known that the olo was only for the use of the chiefs; none of the common people used it. They used the a-la-ia, which was made of koa, or ulu. Its length and width were similar to the olo, except in thickness, it being but of one and a half or two inches thick along the center.

BREAKERS

The line of breakers is the place where the outer surf rises and breaks at deep sea. This is called the *kulana nalu*. Any place nearer or closer in where the surf rises and breaks again, as they sometimes do, is called the *ahua*, known also as *kipapa* or *puao*.

There are only two kinds of surf in which riding is indulged; these are called the *kakala*, known also as *lauloa*, or long surf, and the *ohu*, sometimes called *opuu*. The former is a surf that rises, covering the whole distance from one end of the beach to the other. These, at times, form in successive waves that roll in with high, threatening crest, finally falling over bodily. The first of a series of surf waves usually partake of this character, and is never taken by a rider, as will be mentioned later. The ohu is a very small comber that rises up without breaking, but of such strength that sends the board on speedily. This is considered the best, being low and smooth, and the riding thereon easy and pleasant, and is therefore preferred by ordinary surf riders. The lower portion of the breaker is called *honua*, or foundation, and the portion near a cresting wave is termed the *muku* side, while the distant, or clear side, as some express it, is known as the *lala*.

SURF COAXING

During calm weather when there was no surf there were two ways of making or coaxing it practiced by the ancient Hawaiians, the generally adopted method being for a swimming party to take several strands of the sea convolvulus vine, and swinging it around the head lash it down unitedly upon the water until the desired result was obtained, at the same time chanting as follows:

Ho ae; ho ae iluna i ka pohuehue,

Ka ipu nui lawe mai.

Ka ipu iki waiho aku.

METHODS OF SURF RIDING

The swimmer, taking position at the line of breakers, waits for the proper surf. As before mentioned the first one is allowed to pass by. It is never ridden, because its front is rough. If the second comber is seen to be a good one it is sometimes taken, but usually the third or fourth one is the best, both from the regularity of its breaking and the foam calmed surface of the sea through the travel of its predecessors.

In riding with the olo or thick board, on a big surf, the board is pointed landward and the rider, mounting it, paddles with his hands and impels with his feet to give the board a forward movement, and when it receives the momentum of the surf and begins to rush downward, the skilled rider will guide his course straight, or obliquely, apparently at will, according to the spending character of the surf ridden, to land himself high and dry on the beach, or dismount on nearing it, as he may elect. This style was called *kipapa*. In using the olo great care had to be exercised in its management, lest from the height of the wave—if coming in direct—the board would be forced into the base of the breaker, instead of floating lightly and riding on the surface of the water, in which case, the wave force being spent, reaction throws both rider and board into the air.

In the use of the olo the rider had to swim out around the line of surf to obtain position, or be conveyed thither by canoe. To swim out through the surf with such a buoyant bulk was not possible, though it was sometimes done with the thin boards, the a-la-ia. These latter are good for riding all kinds of surf, and are much easier to handle than the olo.

Various positions used to be indulged in by old-time experts in this aquatic sport, such as standing, kneeling and sitting. These performances could only be indulged in after the board had taken on the surf momentum and in the following manner. Placing the hands on each side of the board, close to the edge, the weight of the body was thrown on the hands, and the feet brought up quickly to the kneeling position. The sitting position is attained in the same way, though the hands must not be removed from the board till the legs are thrown forward and the desired position is secured. From the kneeling to the standing position was obtained by placing both hands again on the board and with agility leaping up to the erect attitude, balancing the body on the swift-coursing board with outstretched hands.

SURF SWIMMING WITHOUT BOARD

Kaha nalu is the term used for surf swimming without the use of the board, and was done with the body only. The swimmer, as with a board, would go out for position and, watching his opportunity, would strike out with hands and feet to obtain headway as the approaching comber with its breaking crest would catch him, and with his rapid swimming powers bear him onward with swift momentum, the body being submerged in the foam; the head and shoulders only being seen. Kaha experts could ride on the *lala* or top of the surf as if riding with a board.

CANOE RIDING—PA-KA WAA

Canoe riding in the surf is another variety of this favorite sport, though not so general, nor perhaps so calculated to win the plaudits of an admiring throng, yet requiring dexterous skill and strength to avoid disastrous results.

Usually two or three persons would enter a canoe and paddle out to the line of breakers. They would pass the first, second, or third surf if they were *kakalas*, it being impossible to shoot such successfully with a canoe, but if an *ohu* is approaching, then they would take position and paddle quickly till the swell of the cresting surf would seize the craft and speed it onward without further aid of paddles, other than for the steersman to guide it straight to shore, but woe be to all if his paddle should get displaced.

Canoe riding has been practiced of late years in mild weather by a number of the Waikiki residents, several of whom are becoming expert in this exciting and exhilarating sport.

APPENDIX F

"A Royal Sport: Surfing at Waikiki," by Jack London

In April 1907 Jack London and his wife, Charmian, sailed out of San Francisco, bound for the South Seas on their yacht, *The Snark*. Their first stop was Honolulu. London's famous account of surfing at Waikīkī appeared that October in *A Woman's Home Companion* and then became a chapter in his widely read travel narrative, *The Cruise of the Snark* (Macmillan, 1911).

That is what it is, a royal sport for the natural kings of earth. The grass grows right down to the water at Waikiki Beach, and within fifty feet of the everlasting sea. The trees also grow down to the salty edge of things, and one sits in their shade and looks seaward at a majestic surf thundering in on the beach to one's very feet. Half a mile out, where is the reef, the white-headed combers thrust suddenly skyward out of the placid turquoise-blue and come rolling into shore. One after another they come, a mile long, with smoking crests, the white battalions of the infinite army of the sea. And one sits and listens to the perpetual roar, and watches the unending procession, and feels tiny and fragile before this tremendous force expressing itself in fury and foam and sound. Indeed, one feels microscopically small, and the thought that one may wrestle with this sea raises in one's imagination a thrill of apprehension, almost of fear. Why, they are a mile long, these bull-mouthed monsters, and they weigh a thousand tons, and they charge in to shore faster than a man can run. What chance? No chance at all, is the verdict of the shrinking ego; and one sits, and looks and listens, and thinks the grass and the shade are a pretty good place in which to be.

JACK LONDON (1876–1916)
PHOTOGRAPHY BY PURDY, 1906;
COURTESY LIBRARY OF CONGRESS,
PRINTS AND PHOTOGRAPHS DIVISION.

And suddenly, out there where a big smoker lifts skyward, rising like a sea-god from out of the welter of spume and churning white, on the giddy, toppling, overhanging and downfalling, precarious crest appears the dark head of a man. Swiftly he rises through the rushing white. His black shoulders, his chest, his loins, his limbs—all is abruptly projected on one's vision. Where but the moment before was only the wide desolation and invincible roar, is now a man, erect, full-statured, not struggling frantically in that wild movement, not buried and crushed and buffeted by those mighty monsters, but standing above them all, calm and superb, poised on the giddy summit, his feet buried in the churning foam, the salt smoke rising to his knees, and all the rest of him in the free air and flashing sunlight, and he is flying through the air, flying forward, flying fast as the surge on which he stands. He is a Mercury—a brown Mercury. His heels are winged, and in them is the swiftness of the sea. In truth, from out of the sea he has leaped upon the back of the sea, and he is riding the sea that roars and bellows and cannot shake him from its back. But no frantic outreaching and balancing is his. He is impassive, motionless as a statue carved suddenly by some miracle out of the sea's depth from which he rose. And straight on toward shore he flies on his winged heels and the white crest of the breaker. There is a wild burst of foam, a long tumultuous rushing sound as the breaker falls futile and spent on the beach at your feet; and there, at your feet, steps calmly ashore a Kanaka, burnt golden and brown by the tropic sun. Several minutes ago he was a speck a quarter of a mile away. He has "bitted the bull-mouthed breaker" and ridden it in, and the pride in the feat shows in the carriage of his magnificent body as he glances for a moment carelessly at you who sit in the shade of the shore. He is a Kanaka—and more, he is a man, a member of the kingly species that has mastered matter and the brutes and lorded it over creation.

And one sits and thinks of Tristram's last wrestle with the sea on that fatal morning; and one thinks further to the fact that Kanaka has done what Tristram never did, and that he knows a joy of the sea that Tristram never knew. And still further one thinks. It is all very well, sitting here in cool shade of the beach, but you are a man, one of the kingly species, and what that Kanaka can do, you can do yourself. Go to. Strip off your clothes that are a nuisance in this mellow clime. Get in and wrestle with the sea; wing your heels with the skill and power that reside in you; bit the sea's breakers, master them, and ride upon their backs as a king should.

And that is how it came about that I tackled surf-riding. And now that I have tackled it, more than ever do I hold it to be a royal sport. But first let me explain the physics of it. A wave is a communicated agitation. The water that composes the body of a wave does not move. If it did, when a stone is thrown into a pond and the ripples spread away in an ever widening circle, there would appear at the center an ever increasing hole. No, the water that composes the body of a wave is stationary. Thus, you may watch a particular portion of the ocean's surface and you will see the same water rise and fall a thousand times to the agitation communicated by a thousand successive waves. Now imagine this communicated agitation moving shoreward. As the bottom shoals, the lower portion of the wave strikes land first and is stopped. But water is fluid, and the upper portion has not struck anything, wherefore it keeps on communicating its agitation, keeps on going. And when the top of the wave keeps on going, while the bottom of it lags behind, something is bound to happen. The bottom of the wave drops out from under and the top of the wave falls over, forward, and down, curling and cresting and roaring as it does so. It is the bottom of a wave striking against the top of the land that is the cause of all surfs.

But the transformation from a smooth undulation to a breaker is not abrupt except where the bottom shoals abruptly. Say the bottom shoals gradually for from quarter of a mile to a mile, then an equal distance will be occupied by the transformation. Such a bottom is that off the beach of Waikiki, and it produces a splendid surf-riding surf. One leaps upon the back of a breaker just as it begins to break, and stays on it as it continues to break all the way in to shore.

And now to the particular physics of surf-riding. Get out on a flat board, six feet long, two feet wide, and roughly oval in shape. Lie down upon it like a small boy on a coaster and paddle with your hands out to deep water, where the waves begin to crest. Lie out there quietly on the board. Sea after sea breaks before, behind, and under and over you, and rushes in to shore, leaving you behind. When a wave crests, it gets steeper. Imagine yourself, on your board, on the face of that steep slope. If it stood still, you would slide down just as a boy slides down a hill on his coaster. "But," you object, "the wave doesn't stand still." Very true, but the water composing the wave stands still, and there you have the secret. If ever you start sliding down the face of that wave, you'll keep on sliding and you'll never reach the bottom. Please

don't laugh. The face of that wave may be only six feet, yet you can slide down it a quarter of a mile, or half a mile, and not reach the bottom. For, see, since a wave is only a communicated agitation or impetus, and since the water that composes a wave is changing every instant, new water is rising into the wave as fast as the wave travels. You slide down this new water, and yet remain in your old position on the wave, sliding down the still newer water that is rising and forming the wave. You slide precisely as fast as the wave travels. If it travels fifteen miles an hour, you slide fifteen miles an hour. As the wave travels, this water obligingly heaps itself into the wave, gravity does the rest, and down you go, sliding the whole length of it. If you still cherish the notion, while sliding, that the water is moving with you, thrust your arms into it and attempt to paddle; you will find that you have to be remarkably quick to get a stroke, for that water is dropping astern just as fast as you are rushing ahead.

And now for another phase of the physics of surf-riding. All rules have their exceptions. It is true that the water in a wave does not travel forward. But there is what may be called the send of the sea. The water in the overtoppling crest does move forward, as you will speedily realize if you are slapped in the face by it, or if you are caught under it and are pounded by one mighty blow down under the surface panting and gasping for half a minute. The water in the top of a wave rests upon the water in the bottom of the wave. But when the bottom of the wave strikes the land, it stops, while the top goes on. It no longer has the bottom of the wave to hold it up. Where was solid water beneath it, is now air, and for the first time it feels the grip of gravity, and down it falls, at the same time being torn asunder from the lagging bottom of the wave and flung forward. And it is because of this that riding a surfboard is something more than a mere placid sliding down a hill. In truth, one is caught up and hurled shoreward as by some Titan's hand.

I deserted the cool shade, put on a swimming suit, and got hold of a surfboard. It was too small a board. But I didn't know, and nobody told me. I joined some little Kanaka boys in shallow water, where the breakers were well spent and small—a regular kindergarten school. I watched the little Kanaka boys. When a likely-looking breaker came along, they flopped upon their stomachs on their boards, kicked like mad with their feet, and rode the breaker in to the beach. I tried to emulate them. I watched them, tried to do everything that they did, and failed utterly. The breaker swept past, and I was not on it. I tried again and again. I kicked twice as madly as they did, and failed. Half a dozen would be around. We would all leap on our boards in front of a good breaker. Away our feet would churn like the stern-wheels of river steamboats, and away the little rascals would scoot while I remained in disgrace behind.

I tried for a solid hour, and not one wave could I persuade to boost me shoreward. And then arrived a friend, Alexander Hume Ford, a globe-trotter by profession, bent ever on the pursuit of sensation. And he had found it at Waikiki. Heading for Australia, he had stopped off for a week to find out if there were any thrills of surf-riding, and he had become wedded to it. He had been at it every day for a month and could not yet see any symptoms of the fascination lessening on him. He spoke with authority.

"Get off that board," he said. "Chuck it away at once. Look at the way you're trying to ride it. If ever the nose of that board hits bottom, you'll be disemboweled. Here, take my board. It's a man's size."

I am always humble when confronted by knowledge. Ford knew. He showed me how properly to mount his board. Then he waited for a good breaker, gave me a shove at the right moment, and started me in. Ah, delicious moment when I felt that breaker grip and fling me! On I dashed, a hundred and fifty feet, and subsided with the breaker on the sand. From that moment I was lost. I waded back to Ford with his board. It was a large one, several inches thick, and weighed all of seventy-five pounds. He gave me advice, much of it. He had had no one to teach him, and all that he had laboriously learned in several weeks he communicated to me in half an hour. I really learned by proxy. And inside of half an hour I was able to start myself and ride in. I did it time after time, and Ford applauded and advised. For instance, he told me to get just so far forward on the board and no farther. But I must have got some farther, for as I came charging in to land, that miserable board poked its nose down to bottom, stopped abruptly, and turned a somersault, at the same time violently severing our relations. I was tossed through the air like a chip and buried ignominiously under the downfalling breaker. And I realized that if it hadn't been for Ford, I'd have been disemboweled. That particular risk is part of the sport, Ford says. Maybe he'll have it happen to him before he leaves Waikiki, and then, I feel confident, his yearning for sensation will be satisfied for a time.

When all is said and done, it is my steadfast belief that homicide is worse than suicide, especially if, in the former case, it is a woman. Ford saved me from being a homicide. "Imagine your legs are a rudder," he said. "Hold them close together, and steer with them." A few minutes later I came charging in on a comber. As I neared the beach, there, in the water, up to her waist, dead in front of me, appeared a woman. How was I to stop that comber on whose back I was? It looked like a dead woman. The board weighed seventy-five pounds, I weighed a hundred and sixty-five. The added weight had a velocity of fifteen miles per hour. The board and I constituted a projectile. I leave it to the physicists to figure out the force of the impact upon that poor, tender woman. And then I remembered my guardian angel, Ford. "Steer with your legs!" rang through my brain. I steered with my legs, I steered sharply, abruptly, with all my legs and with all my might. The board sheered around broadside on the crest. Many things happened simultaneously. The wave gave me a passing buffet, a light tap as the taps of waves go, but a tap sufficient to knock me off the board and smash me down through the rushing water to bottom, with which I came in violent collision and upon which I was rolled over and over. I got my head out for a breath of air and then gained my feet. There stood the woman before me. I felt like a hero. I had saved her life. And she laughed at me. It was not hysteria. She had never dreamed of her danger. Anyway, I solaced myself, it was not I but Ford that saved her, and I didn't have to feel like a hero. And besides, that leg-steering was great. In a few minutes more of practice I was able to thread my way in and out past several bathers and to remain on top of my breaker instead of going under it.

"Tomorrow," Ford said, "I am going to take you out into the blue water."

I looked seaward where he pointed, and saw the great smoking combers that made the breakers I had been riding look like ripples. I don't know what I might have said had I not recollected just then that I was one of a kingly species. So all that I did say was, "All right, I'll tackle them tomorrow."

The water that rolls in on Waikiki Beach is just the same as the water that laves the shores of all the Hawaiian Islands; and in ways, especially from the swimmer's standpoint, it is wonderful water. It is cool enough to be comfortable, while it is warm enough to permit a swimmer to stay in all day without experiencing a chill. Under the sun or the stars, at high noon or at midnight, in midwinter or in midsummer, it does not matter when, it is always the same temperature—not too warm, not too cold, just right. It is wonderful water, salt as old ocean itself, pure and crystal-clear. When the nature of the water is considered, it is not so remarkable after all that the Kanakas are one of the most expert of swimming races.

So it was, next morning, when Ford came along, that I plunged into the wonderful water for a swim of indeterminate length. Astride of our surfboards, or, rather, flat down upon them on our stomachs, we paddled out through the kindergarten where the little Kanaka boys were at play. Soon we were out in deep water where the big smokers came roaring in. The mere struggle with them, facing them, and paddling seaward over them and through them, was sport enough in itself. One had to have his wits about him, for it was a battle in which mighty blows were struck, on one side, and in which cunning was used on the other side—a struggle between insensate force and intelligence. I soon learned a bit. When a breaker curled over my head, for a swift instant I could see the light of day through its emerald body; then down would go my head, and I would clutch the board with all my strength. Then would come the blow, and to the onlooker on shore I would be blotted out. In reality the board and I have

passed through the crest and emerged in the respite of the other side. I should not recommend those smashing blows to an invalid or delicate person. There is weight behind them, and the impact of the driven water is like a sandblast. Sometimes one passes through half a dozen combers in quick succession, and it is just about that time that he is liable to discover new merits in the stable land and new reasons for being on shore.

Out there in the midst of such a succession of big smoky ones, a third man was added to our part, one Freeth. Shaking the water from my eyes as I emerged from one wave and peered ahead to see what the next one looked like, I saw him tearing in on the back of it, standing upright on his board, carelessly poised, a young god bronzed with sunburn. We went through the wave on the back of which he rode. Ford called to him. He turned an airspring from his wave, rescued his board from its maw, paddled over to us and joined Ford in showing me things. One thing in particular I learned from Freeth, namely, how to encounter the occasional breaker of exceptional size that rolled in. Such breakers were really ferocious, and it was unsafe to meet them on top of the board. But Freeth showed me, so that whenever I saw one of that caliber rolling down on me, I slid off the rear end of the board and dropped down beneath the surface, my arms over my head and holding the board. Thus, if the wave ripped the board out of my hands and tried to strike me with it (a common trick of such waves), there would be a cushion of water a foot or more in depth, between my head and the blow. When the wave passed, I climbed upon the board and paddled on. Many men have been terribly injured, I learn, by being struck by their boards.

The whole method of surf-riding and surf-fighting, I learned, is one of nonresistance. Dodge the blow that is struck at you. Dive through the wave that is trying to slap you in the face. Sink down, feet first, deep under the surface, and let the big smoker that is trying to smash you go by far overhead. Never be rigid. Relax. Yield yourself to the waters that are ripping and tearing at you. When the undertow catches you and drags you seaward along the bottom don't struggle against it. If you do, you are liable to be drowned, for it is stronger than you. Yield yourself to that undertow. Swim with it, not against it, and you will find the pressure removed. And, swimming with it, fooling it so that it does not hold you, swim upward at the same time. It will be no trouble at all to reach the surface.

The man who wants to learn surf-riding must be a strong swimmer, and he must be used to going under the water. After that, fair strength and common sense are all that is required. The force of the big comber is rather unexpected. There are mix-ups in which board and rider are torn apart and separated by several hundred feet. The surf-rider must take care of himself. No matter how many riders swim out with him, he cannot depend upon any of them for aid. The fancied security I had in the presence of Ford and Freeth made me for-

get that it was my first swim out in deep water among the big ones. I recollected, however, and rather suddenly, for a big wave came in, and away went the two men on its back all the way to shore. I could have been drowned a dozen different ways before they got back to me.

One slides down the face of a breaker on his surfboard, but he has to get started to sliding. Board and rider must be moving shoreward at a good rate before the wave overtakes them. When you see the wave coming that you want to ride in, you turn tail to it and paddle shoreward with all your strength, using what is called the windmill stroke. This is a sort of spurt performed immediately in front of the wave. If the board is going fast enough, the wave accelerates it, and the board begins its quarter-of-a-mile slide.

I shall never forget the first big wave I caught out there in the deep water. I saw it coming, turned my back on it, and paddled for dear life. Faster and faster my board went, till it seemed my arms would drop off. What was happening behind me I could not tell. One cannot look behind and paddle the windmill stroke. I heard the crest of the wave hissing and churning, and then my board was lifted and flung forward. I scarcely knew what happened the first half-minute. Though I kept my eyes open, I could not see anything, for I was buried in the rushing white of the crest. But I did not mind. I was chiefly conscious of ecstatic bliss at having caught the wave. At the end of the half-minute, however, I began to see things, and to breathe. I saw that three feet of the nose of my board was clear out of water and riding on the air. I shifted my weight forward, and made the nose come down. Then I lay, quite at rest in the midst of the wild movement, and watched the shore and the bathers on the beach grow distinct. I didn't cover quite a quarter of a mile on that wave, because, to prevent the board from diving, I shifted my weight back, but shifted it too far and fell down the rear slope of the wave.

It was my second day at surf-riding, and I was quite proud of myself. I stayed out there four hours, and when it was over, I was resolved that on the morrow I'd come in standing up. But that resolution paved a distant place. On the morrow I was in bed. I was not sick, but I was very unhappy, and I was in bed. When describing the wonderful water of Hawaii I forgot to describe the wonderful sun of Hawaii. It is a tropic sun, and, furthermore, in the first part of June, it is an overhead sun. It is also an insidious, deceitful sun. For the first time in my life I was sunburned unawares. My arms, shoulders, and back had been burned many times in the past and were tough; but not so my legs. And for four hours I had exposed the tender backs of my legs, at right angles, to that perpendicular Hawaiian sun. It was not until after I got ashore that I discovered the sun

had touched me. Sunburn at first is merely warm; after that it grows intense and the blisters come out. Also, the joints, where the skin wrinkles, refuse to bend. That is why I spent the next day in bed. I couldn't walk. And that is why, today, I am writing this in bed. It is easier to than not to. But tomorrow, ah, tomorrow, I shall be out in that wonderful water, and I shall come in standing up, even as Ford and Freeth. And if I fail tomorrow, I shall do it the next day, or the next. Upon one thing I am resolved: the *Snark* shall not sail from Honolulu until I, too, wing my heels with the swiftness of the sea, and become a sunburned, skin-peeling Mercury.

CHAPTER ONE

1. King in Cook 1784, 3:147
2. London, Jack 1911, 79–82

CHAPTER TWO

1. Morrison 1935, 226
2. Ellis 1831, 1:305

CHAPTER THREE

1. Byron 1826, 97
2. Stewart 1839, 196
3. King in Cook 1784, 3:145–147
4. Fornander 1916–1920, 4:112–125
5. Westervelt 1915, 52–54
6. Taylor 1958, 20
7. Thrum 1896, 106–107
8. Haleole 1919, 446–458

9. Kalakaua 1888, 229–246
10. Ellis 1831, 4:371
11. Pukui 1949, 255–256
12. Westervelt 1915, 157–172
13. Caton 1880, 243–244
14. Thrum 1896, 109
15. Malo 1915, 56–57
16. Malo 1951, 223
17. Fornander 1880, 2:96
18. Fornander 1916–1920, 6:206–207
19. Emory 1933, 144
20. Stokes 1919; 1991, 67–70

CHAPTER FOUR

1. Jarves 1884, 298; Bates 1854, 298; Boddam-Whetham 1876, 120; Nordhoff 1874, p. 52
2. Ruschenberger 1838, 2:373

3. Bingham 1847, 136–137
4. Dibble 1909, 102
5. Emerson 1892, 59
6. Adams 1930, 59
7. Emerson 1892, 59

CHAPTER FIVE

1. Mark Twain 1872, 526
2. London, Charmian 1922, 94
3. Ford 1911, 143–144
4. Ford 1909, 17
5. London, Jack 1922, 8
6. London, Charmian 1922, 312

Books and articles cited in the text are listed below, along with research publications on surfing by Ben Finney, which include more extensive documentation than given here.

Adams, Henry.
1930   *Letters of Henry Adams.*
        Boston: Houghton Mifflin.

Andrews, Lorrin.
1865   *A Dictionary of the Hawaiian Language.*
        Honolulu: H. M. Whitney.

Bates, George W. ["A Haole"].
1854   *Sandwich Island Notes.*
        New York: Harper & Bros.

Beaglehole, John C., ed.
1967   *The Voyage of the Resolution
        and the Discovery, 1776–1780,*
        vols. 1 and 2. Cambridge:
        Hakluyt Society.

Bingham, Hiram.
1847   *A Residence of Twenty-one Years
        in the Sandwich Islands.*
        New York: Converse.

Boddam-Whetham, John W.
1876   *Pearls of the Pacific.*
        London: Hurst and Blackett.

Byron, Captain, the Rt. Hon. Lord.
1826   *Voyage of HMS Blonde
        to the Sandwich Islands.*
        London: J. Murray.

Caton, John D.
1880.   *Miscellanies.*
        Boston: Houghton, Osgood.

Cook, James, and James King.
1784   *A Voyage to the Pacific Ocean . . . ,*
        vols. 1–3. London:
        G. Nicholl and T. Cadell.

Dibble, Sheldon.
1909   *A History of the Sandwich Islands.*
        Honolulu: T. G. Thrum

Ellis, William.
1831   *Polynesian Researches,* vols. 1–3.
        London: Fisher, Son, & Jackson.

Emerson, Nathaniel B.
1892   "Causes of Decline of Ancient
        Polynesian Sports." *The Friend,*
        vol. 50, no. 8, 57–60.
1909   *The Unwritten Literature of Hawaii.*
        Washington: Bureau of American
        Ethnology Bulletin 38.

Emory, Kenneth.
1933   "Sports, Games, and Amusements."
        In *Ancient Hawaiian Civilization,*
        edited by Helen Pratt. Honolulu: The
        Kamehameha Schools.

Finney, Ben.
1959a   "Hawaiian Surfing: A Study in
        Cultural Change." M.A. Thesis,
        University of Hawai‘i.
1959b   "Surfboarding in Oceania:
        Its Pre-European Distribution."
        *Wiener Völkerkundliche
        Mitteilungen,* 2:23–36.
1959c   "Surfing in Ancient Hawai‘i."
        Journal of the Polynesian Society,
        68:327–347.
1960   "The Development and Diffusion
        of Modern Hawaiian Surfing." *Journal
        of the Polynesian Society,* 69:315–331.
1962   "Surfboarding in West Africa." *Wiener
        Völkerkundliche Mitteilungen, 5:41–42.*

Ford, Alexander Hume.
1909   "Riding the Surf in Hawaii." *Collier's
        National Weekly,* 42:17.
1911   "Out-door Allurements."
        Thrum's Hawaiian Annual, 143–149.

Fornander, Abraham.
1878, 1880, 1885
    An Account of the Polynesian Race:
    Its Origin and Migrations, vols. 1–3.
    London: Trübner. (Reprinted 1969,
    Tokyo and Rutland, Vt.: Tuttle).
1916–1920
    Fornander Collection of Hawaiian Antiquities
    and Folklore. Translated and edited by
    Thomas G. Thrum. Honolulu: Memoirs
    of the Bernice P. Bishop Museum,
    vols. 4–6.

Haleole.
1919   "The Hawaiian Romance of Laieikawai."
    Translated and edited by Martha W.
    Beckwith. *Thirty-Third Annual Report*
    of the Bureau of American Ethnology . . .
    1911–1912. Washington:
    Smithsonian Institution, 285–666.

Hawaiian Ethnological Notes
Various dates
    A collection of manuscript notes by various
    authors in the library of the Bernice P.
    Bishop Museum, Honolulu.

Iʻi, John Papa.
1959   *Fragments of Hawaiian History*. Translated by
    Mary Kawena Pukui; edited by Dorothy B.
    Barrère. Honolulu: Bishop Museum Press.

Jarves, James J.
1844   *Scenes and Scenery in the Sandwich Islands*.
    London: Edward Moxon.

Kalakaua, David.
1888   *The Legends and Myths of Hawaii.*
    New York: C.L. Webster.

Kamakau, Samuel Manaiakalani.
1976   *The Works of the People of Old*
    (Na Hana a ka Poʻe Kahiko).
    Translated by Mary Kawena Pukui;
    edited by Dorothy B. Barrère.
    Honolulu: Bishop Museum Press.

London, Charmian.
1922   *Our Hawaii.*
    New York: Macmillan.

London, Jack.
1911   *The Cruise of the Snark.*
    New York: Macmillan.
1922   "My Hawaiian Aloha," as a preface to
    Our Hawaii, by Charmian London.
    New York: Macmillan.

Malo, David.
1951   *Hawaiian Antiquities (Moʻolelo Hawaiʻi).*
    Translated by Nathaniel B. Emerson. 2d ed.
    Bernice P. Bishop Museum
    Special Publication 2.
    Honolulu: Bishop Museum.

Mark Twain.
1872   *Roughing It.*
    Chicago: F. G. Gilman.

Morrison, James.
1935   *The Journal of James Morrison,*
    Boatswain's Mate on the Bounty.
    London: Golden Cockerel Press.

Nordhoff, Charles.
1874   *Northern California, Oregon, and the*
    Sandwich Islands.
    New York: Harper.

Pukui, Mary Kawena.
1949   "Songs (meles) of Old Kaʻu , Hawaii."
    Journal of American Folklore, vol. 62,
    no. 245, 247–258.

Pukui, Mary Kawena, Samuel H. Elbert,
    and Esther T. Mookini.
1974   *Place Names of Hawaiʻi.*
    Honolulu: University of Hawaiʻi Press.

Pukui, Mary Kawena, and Samuel H. Elbert.
1986   *Hawaiian Dictionary.*
    Rev. ed. Honolulu:
    University of Hawaiʻi Press.

Ruschenberger, William Samuel W.
1838   *Narrative of a Voyage Round the World.*
    London: Richard Bentley.

Stewart, Charles Samuel.
1839   *A Residence in the Sandwich Islands.*
    Boston: Weeks, Jordan & Co.

Stokes, John F. G.
1919   *Heiaus of Hawaii.*
    Manuscript in the Bernice P. Bishop
    Museum, Honolulu.
1991   *Heiau of the Island of Hawaiʻi: A Historic*
    Survey of Native Hawaiian Temple Sites,
    edited by Tom Dye. Bishop Museum
    Bulletin in Anthropology 2.
    Honolulu: Bishop Museum.

Taylor, Clarice.
1958   "Tales About Hawaii."
          Honolulu Star-Bulletin, November 26:20.

Thrum, Thomas G., ed.
1896   "Hawaiian Surf Riding"
          (by an anonymous Hawaiian author from
          Kona, Hawai'i), with an introduction by T.
          G. Thrum and translated by M. K. Nakuina
          and T. G. Thrum. *Thrum's Hawaiian Annual*
          for 1896, 106–113.

Westervelt, William D.
1915   *Legends of Old Honolulu.*
          Boston: George H. Ellis.